NO LONGER PROPERTY OF
SEATTLE PUBLIC LIBRARY

ON PURPOSE

The Power *of* Authenticity and Intention

D1572622

YVETTE R. SIMPSON, ESQ./MBA

ILLUSTRATIONS BY
JOSEPH R. HOFFECKER

MINDSTIR MEDIA

On Purpose
Copyright © 2023 by Yvette R. Simpson, Esq./MBA. All rights reserved.

No part of this book may be used or reproduced in any manner whatsoever without written permission, except in the case of brief quotations embodied in critical articles and reviews. For more information, e-mail all inquiries to info@mindstirmedia.com.

Published by Mindstir Media, LLC
45 Lafayette Rd | Suite 181| North Hampton, NH 03862 | USA
1.800.767.0531 | www.mindstirmedia.com

Printed in the United States of America
ISBN: 978-1-960142-30-6

ACKNOWLEDGMENTS

To my husband, my bwana, Joe Hoffecker, who is my rock, my encourager, my greatest cheerleader. I love you, honey.

To our girls, who motivate my work to make the world a better place for them and future generations.

To my Grandma Pearl, whose wisdom I didn't fully appreciate until I was older and whose sacrifice is the reason I'm here.

To my sister, who is the sugar to my spice, who gives herself so generously to her true purpose of being a caregiver, mother, and grandmother. She inspires me every day. She raised three strong boys, my nephews, who are now young men in a world where doing that seems impossible. They are like sons to me and, like our girls, are my motivation for changing the world for the better.

To so many great friends, adopted moms and mentors and proteges and adopted children who taught me so many essential life lessons, even when I thought I was the one teaching.

CONTENTS

INTRODUCTION

I AM.

I am from Zone 15, the "one-five," the real ones say it like that. Black Mecca, the Village of Lincoln Heights, Ohio, once a Black Wall Street, destroyed by hate and racism.

I am from a village on a street named LOVE—God's way of showing me I had everything I needed.

I am from Double Dutch and ice balls, caramel apples, pigtails, and "Girl, you better get in before the streetlights come on."

I am from the struggle, and love, and hurt, and healing, and brokenness, and words unspoken and laughter to bridge the divide.

I am from we eat the pig from the rootah to the tootah because we made the most of what we had, potato salad, collard greens, chicken five ways, and peach cobbler.

I am from Ms. Pearl's house, where everyone is welcome.

I am from southpaw, and "No, I'm not using the right-handed scissors" to "I may be the first, but I won't be the last."

I am from Pastor Uncle, and you never miss church, to spending Sunday School offering on penny candy.

I am from first to graduate college to more graduations than my father could stand.

I am from getting out, moving up, and changing the world, leaving it better than I found it.

Welcome to my world. I share the poem I wrote above to show you my heart right from the start. I wrote this book to share the backstory of that poem. It's been birthed in the possibility that the journey I've been on for the past forty-four years—the good, the bad, the successes, and the failures—that all of it was **on purpose.** That there are lessons others can learn from that might provide comfort or assurance to people as they navigate their own lives.

I still see myself as that "little black girl from the projects with a mentally ill mother and drug-addicted father who was raised by her grandmother," who still has so much to learn. And in some ways, I am and always will be. But I am so much more.

Good friends who've lived through my life stories with me convinced me that my story can help others and that it needs to be heard. I believe I was born to help people change the world, so this invitation was one I couldn't resist. I believe it is one more step in my journey of living on purpose.

I consider myself more of a speaker than a writer, so writing a book was a stretch for me. I gave a TEDx Talk in October 2021 about living a purpose-driven life and reinventing yourself, two things I have plenty of experience with. I found that experience—the vulnerable act of sharing a painful and difficult story, opening myself up, and letting people see my insides—to be surprisingly life-giving. Afterward, I began speaking more, especially to emerging and executive leaders, and I realized quickly that what I was sharing was relevant to people. After my speeches, attendees shared with me that my words, my story, meant so much to them.

They felt a connection to my experiences and found my advice useful and hopeful. The realization that my life experiences, my journey, and the lessons that have flowed from it, were somehow impactful to others was motivating, especially for a purpose-driven person like me. So, I decided to take the leap to reinvent myself once again, this time as an author, to take a chance, believing that I have a story worth telling.

This book was birthed in the midst of a once-in-a-generation global pandemic. It's the culmination of a life's journey in pursuit of fulfillment, the kind of fulfillment that can only come from waking up every day living a life that feels real, authentic, doing work that lifts you up and makes you feel more connected to who you are and putting your head on your pillow every night knowing that you gave your all to make the world better. That fulfillment becomes a Holy Grail, something that keeps you in search of it, not sure if you will ever find the real thing or experience it completely. But the pursuit is so essential and the journey so meaningful that it feels worth it.

> The definition of *purpose* is: "The reason for which something is done or created or for which something exists."

Living on purpose means two very different yet interconnected things. One feeds the other and vice versa. In one respect, living on purpose is about living a life that is purpose-filled. It's when your time, energy, effort, and experience at home, work, and in the community are tied to your *purpose*.

The definition of *purpose* is: "The reason for which something is done or created or for which something exists." To be sure, purpose is an individual thing. We all have something, maybe several somethings, we are meant to do. It's your reason for being, your North Star.

Perhaps you were meant to be a mother. Or maybe a mentor. Your North Star could be teaching or medicine. It's important not to confuse the word purpose with career. There are people whose purpose is teaching who don't work in a classroom, yet they teach in other ways and in different places. This book will help you discover your purpose.

The second definition of *purpose* is: "Having as one's intention or objective." Living life on purpose is also about living your life intentionally, owning your power to decide how you spend your time, talent, resources, and energy. So

> The second definition of *purpose* is: "Having as one's intention or objective."

many of us believe that life just happens to us or that we don't have control over the decisions we make or how we live.

The truth is we control more than we think. And we always control how we react to circumstances we don't directly control. Because of this, I challenge leaders to wake up and do something different, in part because it gets them out of their routine; this can shift their perspective and change their direction in a needed way.

But doing something different also reminds us that we choose what we do and what we don't do, which means we can make different choices, or in some cases, choose to do nothing at all. The power to make choices is key to living a purpose-driven life. The false belief that we must do what is safe, lucrative, needed, or dictated is the reason so many people live unfulfilled lives.

It's also why our world is out of balance in so many ways. Choosing to do something inconsistent with your purpose creates a void—your gifts aren't being used where they are most needed. What's more, if you aren't truly fulfilled in the work you are doing, you may not be operating optimally in their current position.

"Don't ask yourself what the world needs. Ask yourself what makes you come alive, and go do that, because what the world needs is people who have come alive" (Howard Thurman).

"Don't ask yourself what the world needs. Ask yourself what makes you come alive, and go do that, because what the world needs is people who have come alive" (Howard Thurman). Give yourself permission to do what your heart desires, what you dream about, and begin to take the very real steps to do it because it is not only what you need but what the world needs as well.

BREAKING UP WITH THE ORDINARY

In 2020, the world changed. A global pandemic, COVID-19, changed everything for so many people around the world. I feel sure it changed me. For three years (and counting), we navigated fear, grief, and loss, shifts in the way we work, how we teach our kids, how we navigate at home, our connection to family and friends, and so much more.

For those who are uncomfortable with change, COVID-19 was jarring, like being poured into a bottle, shaken, and then poured out again. For those used to working in a traditional work environment, where you drove to an office for a day's worth of work, working from home resulted in a seismic shift for so many. Add to that having the kids at home, and you have yet another major adjustment.

That's why millions of women left the workforce, many of whom won't return, at least not in a traditional sense.[1] Millions of people at the peak of their careers, professionals between the ages of thirty and forty-five, left the workplace in search of something new.[2] The pandemic birthed a transition to "remote work" and a new, more permanent model, "hybrid work," where employees have a mixed schedule of working in the office and at home.[3]

As for me, I was already working in a remote environment when the pandemic began. So that shift wasn't as impactful for me as it was for others. But pre-pandemic, I'd traveled several times a month. When restrictions curbed my travel dramatically, it was an adjustment; on the positive side, I was at home more, which helped me reclaim so much time.

In that space, several new passions and purposes were birthed. I've never been a bread person, so while others made sourdough bread, I started making wine and began studying for my wine educator's license. While others tried the latest TikTok craze, I started studying for my realtor's license.

WHEN "NORMAL" ISN'T NORMAL ANYMORE

I was trying desperately to find normalcy in a space and time far from normal. Reminders of death and illness became the norm. And it hit us where we hurt. My own father died after a long battle with cancer. A week later, our dog, Suzie, died. The following year, my mother died unexpectedly of cardiac failure.

---

[1] [National Women's Law Center calculations based on BLS, historical data for Establishment Data Table B-5, available at https://www.bls.gov/webapps/legacy/cesbtab5.htm.]

[2] [https://www.forbes.com/sites/bryanrobinson/2021/06/11/the-great-resignation-migration-and-what-this-means-for-your-career/?sh=62ac1da969aa]

[3] [https://www.shrm.org/executive/resources/articles/pages/executives-weigh-in-on-hybrid-work.aspx]

So many people lost loved ones during this time, some to COVID-19, and others, like me, lost loved ones during the lockdown, which brought its own share of challenges and heartbreak. It was emotionally destabilizing to be unable to visit my mother at her locked-down nursing facility for over a year before she died. Then the following year, we had to limit the number of people visiting my father while he was in hospice.

Planning two funerals in the midst of a pandemic raised even more challenges. Coping with that at a time marked by so much global grief was a real struggle.

Being so close to death prompts deep thinking—about life, and time, the fragility and limitations of it all. Millions of people lost their lives, and tens of millions changed careers or left the workforce altogether. Businesses shuttered, schools closed as education moved into the home, as parents became teachers.

We all became doctors, nurses, and epidemiologists. For those who were already struggling or on the edge psychologically, the pandemic was the straw that broke the camel's back. People with few resources or support found themselves needing even more at a time when resources were significantly limited. We adjusted so much about the way we do things. Masks on airplanes, hand sanitizer everywhere, social distancing.

For what it's worth, I personally welcomed many of these practices, making them part of my regular routine. We adopted a vocabulary and a cadence that was once unfamiliar but quickly became commonplace. Video conferencing and pajamas as pants became the norm as we converted to virtual happy hours and waiting in the Zoom room and sharing through a chat box.

I truly believe that when major, life-altering things happen, the universe is telling us to stop and pay attention. So, looked at this way, what was the global pandemic signaling to us?

In a way, the universe was presenting us a life-giving *opportunity*. On the heels of so much loss, so much grief, so much change, we're invited to take a beat—to look at our lives and decide what, if anything, we want to do differently.

So many I've spoken to shared that the pandemic, the global shutdown, was the first time they had taken a moment to breathe—what with our 24/7 news cycle, constant connection to the world through our cell phones and social media. And that breath, that beat, gave them the space to take notice and take stock of what is most important and what needed to change in their lives.

We have an opportunity here to take the lesson and leave the hurt from this pandemic. It shouldn't take a shutdown for you to take a beat. I want to challenge you to take this opportunity to decide to live **on purpose.**

What does that mean? Living on purpose is, at its foundation, about living authentically, as your true and full self, doing what makes you come alive, and doing so intentionally, not automatically or reactively. Living on purpose isn't quick or easy, but throughout this book, we will take the journey together. I'll be right here with you, guiding you through it.

Living on purpose doesn't mean we all need to blow up our lives overnight; that isn't practical or wise. But what if we each took the time to really think, in ways we rarely do, about how we spend our days—those precious grains of sand in the hourglass?

So many people did just that and decided to leave their jobs and do something completely different; others realized they loved what they were doing, but they wanted to do it differently. Some figured out they are right where they belong and are moving forward even more sure and grateful for the confirmation.

It starts with understanding the two keys to living on purpose, what I call the two L's of purposeful living—lifestyle and legacy.

THE TWO L'S OF LIVING LIFE ON PURPOSE

LEGACY (IMPACT)

YOLO—"YODO"

You've heard the saying, "you only live once." You know, "YOLO?" Well, the truth is you only die once. You live every day.

Legacy is about how we spend those days. It's the significance of the dash between the dates on a headstone. Legacy is about how we will be remembered. As an attorney, I'm aware that the legal definition of *legacy* is largely a monetary concern, specifically the "money or property left to someone in a will." It is also any "thing handed down by a predecessor." But in practice, the word legacy has been used to describe something much bigger than money, the intangible "gifts" we impart to those we love or to humanity.

While legacy can be a big, intimidating word, it gets to the essence of who we are as human beings. It's about making a mark. Letting all the world know "I was here." I mean, who wants to live on this earth and leave it the same way it was when we got here? Of course, not every legacy is a gift. Plenty of people live destructive and depleting lives, destroying or taking far more than they've contributed. But it's fair to say that most of us leave some kind of lasting legacy. The question is, what will it be?

Audre Lorde said, "I work with the consciousness of death at my shoulder, not constantly, but often enough to leave a mark upon all my life's decisions and actions. And it does not matter whether this death comes next week or thirty years from now; this consciousness gives my life another breadth. It helps shape the words I speak, the way I love, my politic of action, the strength of my vision and purpose, the depth of my appreciation of living."

It's beautiful to think about making a contribution, making a difference, and leaving things better than we found them. So after a world-changing pandemic that cost millions of lives, upended families, and devastated finances, let's take stock of our lives, think about how we spend our moments, and consider making a shift. I think we will be better for it. It may well be the silver lining of this otherwise catastrophic event that reshaped our generation.

> Legal definition of *legacy* is largely a monetary concern, specifically the "money or property left to someone in a will." It is also any "thing handed down by a predecessor."

The Journey of Rediscovery

Living a life of purpose is a journey, not a destination. It's not a place you go to, and once you're there, you're done.

Now that you've decided to consider your legacy, where do you start? I'd invite you to take a journey, what I call the "journey of rediscovery." This journey requires three things: You have to go back, you have to go forward, and then you have to go through. It's not uncommon to go through a process of rediscovery, even if you don't recognize that's what you're doing.

When someone is in a crisis, when they lose someone they love, when they are changing homes, relocating, or looking toward retirement, they go through a process of thinking about their past and how they got to where they are at that particular point in their lives. But this process doesn't have to just happen during points of major transition. Instead, we should regularly think about the things that brought us to our current place, our successes and mistakes, our triumphs, our failures, and the lessons we learned from all of it.

> This journey requires three things: You have to go back, you have to go forward, and then you have to go through.

Years ago, I began the practice of revisiting my past annually, usually at the end of the year, before I set my goals for the new year. Some people do this on their birthdays or on the anniversary of a major milestone, perhaps the day you started your career or got married. The date matters less than the discipline of consistent practice.

Because I journal, I usually spend time going through my old journals. I don't read every entry, but I randomly grab journals and read passages from them. I reflect on the things I prayed for that I didn't get, which in most cases are blessings. I recall the things I was grateful for when I had less than I have now. I revisit my dreams, the things I wanted to accomplish.

It's interesting and enlightening to recall the frustrations you had when you were twenty years old when you're forty. I both marvel at how wise I was back then and how simple my problems seemed, and I'm refreshed by all the struggles I worked through. Sometimes I feel envious of how much more optimistic and possible the world seemed when I was younger.

Looking Back to Grow Forward

George Bernard Shaw said, "Youth is wasted on the young," and in many ways that is true. I often wonder what it would be like to live life in reverse. A rediscovery journey allows the chance to do that.

As I go back through my journals, I realize how little I have changed over the years in important ways. For instance, I am reminded that I have always had big dreams and wanted to make a big impact on the world. I have always been a leader and for most of my life been unapologetic, bold, and "fear-less." I have always believed my life would get better and remained hopeful, even when things were at their worst. I have always been a person of strong faith, though part of it was survival instinct.

Are you someone who journals or otherwise keeps track of goals, dreams, and accomplishments? If not, this is a good practice to start now. You will benefit in the future from the wisdom of your present self (which will someday be your past).

We have all encountered people, some very successful, who don't seem grounded. They question themselves, their purpose, their identity, and their motivation constantly. Rarely do they reflect deeply, and they don't seem self-aware. Some may consider these people flaky, shallow, or flighty.

The antidote for this is to do the work. To take the time and go to the places we often want to avoid. This isn't easy. But facing yourself, looking into your dark places, sharpening your rough edges, and examining your blind spots is the work. It's only by looking at yourself deeply and honestly that you can make the changes necessary to get better.

Let's do that now, together. Take a few moments now to reflect on some of the most important, most formative moments of your life. You don't need to write down every detail at this stage unless you feel led to do that. You can just write down instances in your life that were impactful and how they shaped you.

JOURNEY OF REDISCOVERY EXERCISE

_____

_____

_____

_____

_____

_____

_____

_____

_____

_____

_____

_____

_____

_____

_____

_____

_____

_____

When we go back on this journey of rediscovery, we almost certainly identify key times or situations that shaped us, those moments when we realized we could do anything. The thing that almost broke us ... almost, but it didn't. The opposing force that motivates you forward the most.

What are those moments? Don't miss them, mark them. For certain, I have saved myself so much pain by recognizing that those lessons from my past are important to my future. We've all likely met the person who seems to never grow ... they are living the same struggle over and over. Like Groundhog Day but without the learning or the lesson.

As **purpose-driven people**, growth and moving forward are essential to our journey. And looking back is the surest way to grow forward and grow through all that life brings.

So, let's start by going back.

Dreamcasting

Revisit Your Eight-Year-Old Self

"That's gonna be me, but I'm gonna be wearing a skirt."

I was eight years old when I decided what I wanted to be. And whether you were eight, eighteen, twenty-eight, or forty-eight, when you first dreamed of what you wanted to be, going back to that place is pivotal to determining your legacy. By going back, you can better understand your original motivation so that you can question, challenge, and test it.

I'll never forget the day. I was young, but also sassy, determined, and headstrong. I was standing in the library with a good friend (we are still friends to this day, actually), and I was holding a book in my hand. It was one of those "I Want to Be" books.

You remember the books that those of us of a certain age read when we were young. They were hard-bound books with a color cover, and the image on the front matched the title. The one I was holding was titled *I Want to Be a Lawyer*.

On the cover, a man in a blue suit stood in front of a judge on the bench. I looked at that cover, and I declared to my friend, God, the universe, and anyone who would listen, "That's gonna be me, but I'm gonna be wearing a skirt." It's funny that this was the way my eight-year-old brain expressed that I wanted to be a lawyer someday, but I believe I was also rejecting the implied limitation that all lawyers were men. As an unapologetic feminist to this day, I believe that "little Yvette" knew that she was going to have to break some glass to reach that goal.

So, I made the declaration. Check. In many ways, saying the words out loud, to the universe, and to anyone who will listen is half the battle. We'll talk later about how the universe responds when we determine our purpose.

The big question in front of me was, how would I accomplish the dream I had just declared? Eight-year-old Yvette was poor and lived in the projects. My mother was mentally ill, my father battled drug and alcohol addiction, and my grandmother was raising me, my sister, and two of my cousins.

How was I going to become a lawyer? How would I make it through high school? Girls like me from backgrounds like mine don't just grow up and become lawyers. But there is something very powerful about dreaming. I believe my dream kept me alive, kept me going, pushing through the many obstacles I faced on the journey from eight to eighteen.

Spoiler Alert: I made it through high school, college, and law school, and I became a lawyer. It wasn't easy. It took a lot of hard work, prayer, and the help of countless mentors and mamas. I graduated from law school, passed the bar exam, and was recruited to join a top law firm.

When Your Dream Isn't Enough

Sounds like success, right? On paper, everything was working better than I could have ever imagined. I was making great money, had good benefits, and had a bright, clear career path ahead of me. There was a lot I liked about practicing law, which is why I still work as a part-time legal adviser today. But I wasn't fulfilled in my work. The money didn't make me happy. It wasn't enough.

I was nearly four years into my legal career when I realized I needed to make a change. I wasn't sure what that change would look like yet, but I knew somehow that there was more to life. I filled my evenings with community activities, many of which I enjoyed more than my day job, but the majority of my time was spent doing something that didn't fulfill me completely.

I knew I needed to find a way to do work that made my heart sing. I had to figure out how to make my profession my passion, how to do good AND do well.

Right about that time, a good friend of mine was recruiting volunteers to join him for a new nonprofit venture he'd recently started in Africa. I looked into the opportunity. I was able to take the time off of work, and I had the money to go, so I thought, "Why not?"

I'd studied international human rights in law school and had missed the opportunity to go to Africa then. I wasn't going to miss my chance to go this time. So I agreed, and in the fall of 2017, I joined a brigade of volunteers with Village Life Outreach Project (VLOP) for two weeks in Tanzania.

I arrived in Tanzania in search of something. My heart was open on this trip. I was already on the journey of rediscovery, really for only the second time in my professional life. I spent the first morning working with young people and headmasters exploring new ways of teaching. Then I co-taught the children's lines and stage directions for a play on how to use mosquito nets to ward off malaria.

In the evenings, I journaled about my passions and skills and how they might come together in a different career path. Another day, I worked with our engineering team to explore methods to clarify and purify drinking water in the morning, then danced with the children in the afternoon until I nearly passed out from exhaustion. I'd dream of what it might feel like to enjoy my work the way I was enjoying my time in Tanzania.

For two weeks, I spent days working with the education, medical, and engineering teams building community, teaching and learning, and exploring long-term solutions for chronic and critical global problems, all while learning from the villagers so many important lessons about my heritage and culture.

In my free moments, I dreamed about how I might translate the experience I was having, giving my entire self to something bigger than myself in Africa to something as meaningful at home. I filled my journal with Venn diagrams and lists of pros and cons. I engaged in deep, life-changing conversations with fellow brigadiers who were generous with their insight and advice.

I took it all in, in a way I had never done before. I had always been a person who'd "play both sides to the middle" [definition: do one thing while exploring or pursuing another]; it's certainly a survival instinct. The poor child in me liked having options, but for most of my life being a lawyer had been my goal. How could I now be considering doing anything different, twenty years after that original dream?

I recall a powerful moment I shared with one of the Tanzanian students during that trip. We had spent the day with a group of brilliant secondary students, answering their questions, swapping the pen-pal letters we'd brought from America, and asking them about their futures.

One young man, whose voice and tall stature I'd recognized from our church visit the week prior, shared his dream with me. I told him how majestic and powerful I thought his singing voice was and asked him whether he planned to use his gift to pursue a future career in the music industry. To be clear, this young man had one of the most beautiful, powerful voices I've ever heard.

He explained that in his country, if he were selected to go to college, he would have to pursue a profession useful in his country, likely engineering or medicine, and that he would be required to work in or near Tanzania. Very few children in Tanzania were able to pursue secondary school, and even fewer were selected to go to college, and going to college was his dream.

I told him that I lived just miles away from one of the top music conservatories in the country and that with a voice like his, he could be the next Pavarotti. I watched his face light up and then his eyes dim. If only he lived in America. I immediately began plotting how to fit his very tall frame into my very small suitcase.

The world would never hear this amazing, gifted young man's voice because he was born in a place that desperately needed engineers and doctors. Over the next few days, I thought about how very real limitations keep us from pursuing the things we want to pursue and the ways we limit *ourselves*, keeping ourselves from doing the things we dream of doing, failing to challenge or remove the barriers or obstacles standing in our way.

Dreaming Again

My time in Tanzania changed my life for the better. When I returned, I couldn't focus on work. I kept thinking about the children I'd encountered and the impact I was able to make while I was there.

After a few weeks, I was pretty sure that I needed to make a career change. Six months later, I was in a new job, reinventing myself again, and starting a new career in higher education. I would later discover that something about my time with the young people of Tanzania unlocked a new dream of helping young people discover and fulfill their purpose. I couldn't help the young man in Tanzania, but perhaps I could help guide young people in America.

> In chasing a profession, I'd misplaced my purpose.

As I was considering making the change, I went back to talk with "little Yvette." I had to know, where did I go wrong? I was so sure that being a lawyer was what I was supposed to do. Twenty years after standing in that library and making my declaration, I had no clue what I was supposed to do.

I remember our conversation well. It's one I have with her whenever I make a shift. I asked her, "Why did we want to be a lawyer in the first place? What was the original motivation?"

She reminded me that our original motivation for becoming a lawyer wasn't about the money, success, or prestige. She'd seen injustice all around her and wanted to use her gifts to change her world and the world for people in her community. "Ah, that's it." In chasing a profession, I'd misplaced my purpose. It happens more than you can imagine.

Once I knew that, I was able to begin dreaming again. This time, I knew what I really needed. Dreaming not about a career, but about how I might fulfill my purpose in different ways.

Unlocking my purpose was essential because **a purpose is big, wide, and long-term.** Purpose is bigger than a profession, a company, or a title. By understanding my purpose, I could use my gifts and talents in many ways, ways that suit me specifically. That one lesson became the guidepost for the next twenty years of my life.

I revisit "little Yvette" often. She serves as a guide for me when I lose my way, returning me always, to my "why." One word of caution, if you are going to talk to your younger self, try to do it in private if you want to avoid unwanted attention!

To discover or rediscover your legacy, you must go back to the time and place when you first dreamed. That may mean recalling the person you were as a child. Childhood is often the time when we are given permission, even encouraged, to dream.

Young people aren't yet weighed down by limitations of time, life, and obligations—a mortgage, children, retirement. They haven't yet acquired the limiting beliefs that come from living life and older age. They truly believe they can do whatever they put their minds to. But dreaming isn't time-bound. We should dream often, releasing us from the boundaries and limitations that we created for ourselves.

> To discover or rediscover your legacy, you must go back to the time and place when youfirst dreamed.

In my work coaching and advising leaders, I help them unlock their power to change the world in small and large ways. It was a mission that was born during my trip to Tanzania and developed over the course of my journey of rediscovery.

A big part of "unlocking your power" is realizing that you have the power. You have the power to decide how you spend every minute, every hour, and every day. We will talk more about intention later. You have the power to decide to take a different path, to do things differently. Understanding that you have that power is key to discovering your legacy.

I want you to take a minute. Right now. When was the last time you dreamed? Where were you? What were you doing? What room were you in? What were you wearing? What did the air smell like? What was happening around you? Any sounds come to mind? How are you feeling in this moment? Happy? Anxious? Hopeful? Close your eyes for a moment to take it all in. Go back to that place in your mind.

When I was in law school, there were times I struggled with the idea of being a lawyer. I had an amazing faculty adviser who asked me questions like, "When was the last time you felt truly happy?" I know, right? We would have these therapy-like sessions where I would try to imagine what I was doing when I felt happy, so I could figure out what I wanted to do with my life, my legal career.

I want you to do that now. If you have never dreamed about what you want to be, this exercise can be especially helpful. And even if you have, it can get you back to the place where you are able to dream again. Dreaming frees you up to begin thinking about what you are meant to be, and in so doing you can rediscover your purpose and get on the path of fulfilling your legacy.

Dreamcasting is the act of dreaming in living color. It requires openness, imagination, and a bit of creativity. Dreamcasting is envisioning your ideal world as if there are no limitations, like we did when we were younger. When I do this in training sessions, I invite participants to write stories on paper, draw with crayons or markers, read it aloud into a voice recorder, or they can build their dream with play dough or sticks and glue.

Dreamcasting works best when you use a method most comfortable for your learning style. Next, you have to imagine your world in 4D and get inside the story using some of the questions I referenced earlier. What does the room feel like? Who is with you? Be as detailed as you can. The process of thinking through these details helps make the dream more real and may reveal clues that are key to uncovering motivation.

When we are kids, we are encouraged to dream. People routinely ask us what we want to be when we grow up and encourage us to explore the vast array of options, from teacher, police officer, firefighter, to doctor. As we get older, we are told to be more practical. Creative or expressive children are hushed, inhibited, and reprimanded in traditional classrooms, which discourages their imagination, gifts, and natural instincts.

By high school, kids are encouraged to think about what they want to be in a different way, often tied to "grown-up" considerations, like making a good living, success, and stability. It's during these years that kids who had previously been encouraged to dream are now told to be realistic. By college, those suggestions become imperatives, with parents and counselors pressuring young adults to make choices not based on their dreams but on societal expectations.

In my career as a college professor and pre-professional adviser, I met with so many young people who were pursuing a career in law, not because it was their passion or purpose but because their parents wanted them to pursue the profession. They had been convinced that a career in law is prestigious, lucrative, and honorable. I agree it can be all those things.

But it isn't for everyone. I watched so many young people lose their spark over the course of their college career and replace it with stoicism and reticence as they molded themselves into the shape of a law student. They spent their precious time and money pursuing a law degree, which is a burden that locks them into the set career pathway even more.

When I left the legal profession after returning from Tanzania, I had conversations with many of my colleagues, most of them expressing well-wishes or even regrets that we wouldn't be working together anymore. A few shared their secret passions with me, cheering me on to do something they couldn't do because life got in the way.

I think of those colleagues whenever I am coaching leaders through this legacy journey today. The idea that they will always wonder whether they could have been or done something different but never took the chance has motivated me when I have reinvented myself. I never want to wait to do something that I am purposed to do. I don't want to let fear, security, or insecurity keep me from fulfilling my purpose and ultimately my legacy. This is why we have to dreamcast many times throughout our lives.

When we settle into a profession, we get comfortable and we justify why that particular career or job is where we need to be, and we get stuck. Stepping back at different stages of your life to revisit your eight-year-old self and giving yourself permission to dream again, maybe to shift, allows us to ensure that we are, as Howard Thurman describes, doing work that makes us come alive, fulfilling our unique purpose in the world.

Let's take a moment now to dreamcast. Use the box below to write or draw or color what your life would look like if there were no limits. Use descriptive words or pictures to express how things around you look, smell, feel, touch, or taste. The more descriptive, the more alive and more real this will feel for you.

When you feel the urge to think about limitations, stop yourself and remember that dreamcasting works best when we put aside practical considerations, fears, or limiting beliefs.

Imagine you are a kid and you have discovered a magic lamp with a genie inside. You can have or experience anything you want, and you have everything at your disposal, no limitations. Your genie will make what you dream come true, so you aren't limited to just three wishes in this scenario.

Starting with a wide, boundless world is the best way to open your heart and mind to what you really desire for yourself, the things that make you come alive, the things that bring you joy.

DREAMCASTING EXERCISE

_____

_____

_____

_____

_____

_____

_____

_____

_____

_____

_____

_____

_____

_____

_____

_____

_____

_____

_____

_____

_____

_____

_____

Legacy Is a Long Game

This legacy journey is not easy. And it isn't a quick fix. It isn't a straight line either. It's taken me years and many fits and starts, reinventing myself many times before I felt I had really discovered my purpose.

When I left the law firm, I went to work for my alma mater, helping them build their very first pre-law program. I also took a 50% pay cut. Yeah, you heard me correctly. Fifty percent less pay. This was especially surprising to my dad, who had worked in a machine shop most of his career and just couldn't understand why someone would spend that much time and money in school just to switch careers and take less money. Did I mention that this is a journey?

Stepping away from the law firm wasn't about money. It was about giving myself the time and space to figure out what I was ultimately supposed to do with my life. It was kind of like the "big chop" haircut some people make when they have just gotten through something difficult or are setting a new course for their lives. You have to let go of the old things that are no longer serving you to make room for the new things. Like many shifts we make on our journey, we don't realize it at the time, but at every step we are learning something that will be necessary for the work we will do later. That was certainly true for me.

I went from a very structured work environment to showing up to my first day of work with the plan I created, no office, no business cards, no set schedule. What I had was a boss who loved my plan, had faith in me, and was prepared to give me the resources, flexibility, and support I needed to be successful. I just had to figure that out and make it happen.

No pressure, right? This role taught me how to spread my wings, take risks, and have an entrepreneurial mindset. I had no idea at the time how much those lessons would serve me in the roles to come.

For five years, I worked to build an amazing program supporting thousands of students who were considering a career in law at Miami University. That work was so significant and precious and felt very much like the work I was able to do with the students of Tanzania.

The program I helped build still exists and knowing that I helped create a legacy at a two-hundred-year-old educational institution is a part of my legacy as well. That role confirmed that my legacy is tied to helping other people accomplish theirs. I love hearing stories about my students and what they are doing now, knowing that in a very small way I was able to be a part of their success stories.

Like the proverbial ripple in the pond, my presence in their lives was a ripple that became the wave that is the collective impact of the work they are each doing in the world.

But my journey didn't end at Miami University. It was just a beginning. Like the trip to Tanzania, my time at Miami, away from the hustle and bustle of law-firm life, gave me time to consider what I might want to do next.

I realized that while I loved creating and building the program, and working with students was very fulfilling, I didn't see university work as my long-term career. I knew someone else would take the mantle from me and keep the program going. I just wasn't 100% sure what would be next for me.

But every part of the journey teaches important lessons that build on one another, helping move you down the path. Every day, I drove from Cincinnati to Oxford and back home again. Since it was a forty-five-minute drive, I used the time to listen to audiobooks about great people.

Hearing the stories of amazingly impactful people helped me realize there was something to this idea of living on purpose. And that purpose isn't about a moment but instead about a journey that leads you through a life fulfilled.

Making (and Scrapping) Plans

So many people don't pursue their dreams because it feels uncertain. Stepping off the secure path into what's less certain can feel intimidating. So many dreams go unfulfilled because of that fear of the unknown. That is completely understandable.

But for those dream-seekers who are willing to take the leap, the reward can be sweet.

It certainly has been that for me. I never considered myself a risk taker. I like the security of a well-planned journey. I am the person who plans our family trips, and details are my best friend. They are like a security blanket for me. But this legacy journey has taught me that often the good stuff is off-road, behind that tree and around that corner.

> I don't advise anyone to jump off the cliff without a parachute. Prepare for the things you can control, but be ready for the many things that are beyond your control.

If you want to go somewhere different, you can't be afraid to veer of the path and take a different road. It's funny that when I have stepped away from the safe, traditional path I have always discovered another path, a road that may lead through a deep forest, leading me to my next destination.

When I work with leaders who are looking to pursue their purpose, I do my best to help them plan for all that might be ahead. And when I chart a new path, I try my best to scenario plan, to think through all the things I might encounter along the way.

I don't advise anyone to jump off the cliff without a parachute. Prepare for the things you can control, but be ready for the many things that are beyond your control. When I started out, I would have never guessed my path would have been anything other than attorney-judge-retire. That was the lawyer's path and the one I was destined for, or so I thought. By allowing myself to step away, to go off-road, I discovered a whole new path, a new and exciting world on the other side.

I didn't realize my first dream wasn't my only dream. Instead, I have been on a purpose journey, one path leading to another and then another. I'm not done dreaming either. There is so much more out there for me to discover and so many more things for me to do. I just have to remain open to the possibilities and when the time comes, go where the journey takes me, and trust that I will arrive exactly where I am supposed to be.

My advice to you if you want to go on this legacy journey, even if you prepared and planned far in advance: get in, buckle up, and get ready for the roller coaster ride. And if you're like me, you've got your hands up, mouth open, and you're screaming with joy the entire way.

> Get in, buckle up, and get ready for the roller coaster ride. And if you're like me, you've got your hands up, mouth open, and you're screaming with joy the entire way.

Look for Open Windows

The work of pursuing your legacy is tough work. There are many fits and starts. So many closed doors. The legacy journey is one of persistence and grit. But on the other side of that struggle, that fortitude may very well be your purpose, your North Star, your "why," the very thing you were created to put your hands and your heart toward.

When I ran for mayor of Cincinnati in 2017, I started that journey fully intending to see it through to the end. I thought that end would be victory. I had served on the Cincinnati City Council for six years, and it felt like the perfect time to make the move. I believed that my leadership was exactly what the city needed at the time.

So, I prayed, consulted with my personal board of advisers, and I decided to jump in with both feet. Over the course of the next year and a half, my team and I rallied, engaged, and worked our hearts out. We won the primary; we lost the general election. I was devastated. I felt like I let myself down and let so many other people down, people who believed in me.

The Closed Door

After the loss, my husband and I took a trip to Mexico. There I took the time to grieve, reset, and consider what was next. I came back home and began the process of applying for jobs. I was optimistic with my background and experience that getting a new role in Cincinnati would allow me to channel my love for the city into a new and exciting role where I could use my gifts for good. Unfortunately, that didn't happen.

I was recruited for positions, would get to the very end of the process, and then be rejected for the role. It happened once, then again, then again. I couldn't believe it. I have a JD and an MBA. I served the city as an elected leader for six years, creating new initiatives to combat homelessness, poverty, human trafficking, and small business development.

Why was I being turned down for roles that I was qualified to fill? A search firm called me after I was turned down for a role and shared that they had never seen someone so qualified rejected for a role.

My term on the city council ended in January 2018, and I wasn't sure what I would do next. I had to do something different. It was clear to me my next opportunity wasn't in Cincinnati. I was going to have to reinvent myself—again—and create my own destiny.

Because I'd grown up poor, I believed I needed a W-2 and benefits to feel safe and secure. But every W-2 door I had pursued was closed to me. I would have to do something different, step outside my comfort zone, chart a new path, and take a chance on me. I was talented, connected, and enterprising. I had a lot going for me.

My challenge: the closed door. The door that kept me locked in, trapped in the past, in my greatest loss. The door that taunted me: "You were supposed to be mayor, now what?"

I told myself so many things during that time. That I wasn't known outside of Cincinnati. That I wasn't special enough to make it as an entrepreneur. That I would go broke and not have enough to support myself.

For months, I let that door taunt me and tell me who I was and what I couldn't do. But thankfully, while looking for and applying for jobs, I also took time to build my plan and "played both sides to the middle."

I connected with friends who'd started their own businesses, seeking their advice and support. I put the building blocks in place. I created a business plan, opened a bank account, created an LLC, hired an accountant, bought business cards, hired a designer for my website.

> When I stopped staring at that closed door, I turned around and saw a big window on the other side of the room. So many of us can't see the open window because we are still staring at the closed door.

One friend shared her draft proposals as a reference, another counseled me on the art and science of billing for my time—quick lesson on that one: the first number you come up with is almost always about 20% too low. But I digress. I put the plan in motion, and after a few months I got my first client.

By May 2018, I was officially a paid consultant. The ultimate lesson, the kicker from that experience? When I stopped staring at that closed door, I turned around and saw a big window on the other side of the room. So many of us can't see the open window because we are still staring at the closed door. We have to let the past go and look ahead to a brighter future. Take the lesson and leave the hurt from our past failures and losses. On the other side of that room was the window that led to a world beyond my wildest dreams.

It is so important to name the things in your life that hold you back, those closed doors that keep you trapped in a place you no longer belong. In naming them, you can face them and then, ultimately, turn away from them. Take a few minutes now to name some of the doors in your life that have closed that you need to turn away from so you can see and experience an open window waiting for you on the other side of the room.

Exercise: Name the doors that are closed in your life that are keeping you from your next opportunity.

"CLOSED DOOR" EXERCISE

_____

_____

_____

_____

_____

_____

_____

_____

_____

_____

_____

_____

_____

_____

_____

_____

_____

_____

_____

_____

_____

_____

_____

LIFESTYLE (FREEDOM)

The second L of living life on purpose is lifestyle. *Lifestyle* is defined as "the way in which a person or group lives." Legacy is about impact; lifestyle is about *freedom*. What if you had the freedom to live and work the way you want to, not in the future but right now?

During the pandemic, so many of us had to adjust to a different way of living. That once-in-a-generation pandemic gave us the chance to stop, assess, and evaluate how things are working in our lives. As a result, millions of people left their jobs, left the workforce, and set a new course.

At one point during the pandemic, millions of workers were leaving the workplace every month. Women, especially, left the workforce in record numbers, seeking more control over their work schedules and working conditions. They left for companies with more workforce flexibility, shifted industries—some in response to industry shutdowns changed employers, and others left to start their own businesses.

> Legacy is about impact; lifestyle is about *freedom*.

This pandemic workforce crisis, which HR experts referred to as "The Great Resignation," was in part about legacy, which we discussed early, and lifestyle. Working remotely, with children at home, industries shut down, business closures and layoffs created a shift that was for some devastating and for others liberating.

Mid-career professionals began to consider how they might spend their lives in a way that served them better. The possibility of a lifestyle that offers support, flexibility, and accommodation suddenly seemed possible as an alternative to the nine-to-five, clock-in, clock-out, report-to-an-office model.

This shift has been coming for a while. The advent of technology promised more efficiency, allowing workers to work smarter, not harder. But instead, technology gave way to "work smarter *and* harder," with technology facilitating 24-7 connectivity, leading people to extra hours, more demands on their time, and burnout.

The fact is your life, your time, and your decisions are all within your control. Not everything is, but those are. Take a moment to appreciate the freedom you have; you control the decisions you make and the way you spend your time.

Every single minute of every day you can decide to do things differently. Those decisions are not without consequence, but it's important for us to know we have agency. We have the power to change our world and the world around us.

Helping people unlock their power to make the changes that will lead to true fulfillment is my superpower. True fulfillment starts with determining what you desire then pinpointing the few critical obstacles that stand in your way and making the necessary changes. I must emphasize the word "critical" here.

Not every obstacle is a critical one, and most are not as difficult to overcome as we think they are. There are some exceptions. If I decide I want to be Beyoncè tomorrow, one significant obstacle might be that I have bad knees and can't dance the way she does.

One flag here: my goal should not be to become Beyoncè. We will talk more about being yourself later in the chapter about authenticity, so hold that thought.

> Helping people unlock their power to make the changes that will lead to true fulfillment is my superpower.

Second flag, we are talking about pursuing "your purpose," so having a dream to be someone else doesn't really fit the bill. I could decide I want to be a dancer, just one that lowers it like it's lukewarm rather than dropping it like it's hot! That would then require me to make some changes, and I must decide if those changes are worth pursuing this dream.

Deciding how you want to live your life, spend your days, hours, and minutes is living on purpose. Assess for yourself what is working and, conversely, what needs to change. That can be as simple as realizing you really don't do your best work in the morning and shifting your workday to do more intense, analytical thought work in the afternoon.

It can be acknowledging you want to have more time with your children, so you need a work environment that provides parental leave and a flexible work schedule. You love to travel, so a remote work environment or a workplace that allows extended or unlimited vacation may be your best bet. We must know what we want, understand what needs to change to make that happen, and be willing to make the change.

Again, there will be trade-offs and consequences for these decisions. Having the lifestyle you want may very well be worth it. The ultimate goal is doing what you are purposed to do in a way that is most authentic to you. Fulfillment is about finding that alignment so every single day you have is being used in a way that serves you most completely.

PURPOSE & REINVENTION

There are times when, to fulfill your purpose, you have to make a shift or pivot, moving from your current career, company, or position to something different. I call that shift "reinvention." I have affectionately been called the "Queen of Reinvention" because I have shifted and pivoted several times in my life and career. My reinvention story, like so many, was unplanned and unexpected but also necessary and life-changing.

From age eight until age twenty-eight, the plan was for me to graduate high school, college, and law school, pass the bar exam, work for a law firm, and live happily ever after. For twenty years, I pursued and achieved my childhood dream. And then everything changed. I was doing great, sophisticated work, making a good living, and had a pathway to future success.

I thought that was enough. It wasn't.

Rather than stay in a career that didn't fulfill me, I decided to take a step away and figure out what was next. I wasn't sure when I left my law firm what my purpose was, but I knew I had to take a step away from the grind of legal practice to give myself a chance to figure it out. So for the next five years I built and managed the first pre-law program for my alma mater, Miami University.

The trip to Tanzania and my work with the students and headmasters there revealed to me I wanted to help shape and guide the future in a significant way. One of my mentors from Miami had connected with me several times over my career, wanting me to come to work at Miami. I called him and told him that I was looking to make a change.

He reached out to several people at the university who had served as mentors, supporters, and cheerleaders for me when I was a student there, and they began to devise a plan to get me there. As fate would have it, the university was looking to create its first prelaw program. They had an alumni donor and a plan to create, post, and fill a director position within the next few months. Perfect. He asked me to consider whether it would be a role I would consider. I told him I would.

Once the position posted, I saw the salary range, and it became clear the job would be a significant pay cut for me. Remember what I said about choices, tradeoffs, and consequences here. Some people don't fully understand that pursuing your purpose could cost you. You may have to sacrifice something for it, and it may take time to make the transition. But not all change is negative.

On the positive side, I would have the freedom to shape and guide the program; I would have a much more flexible schedule than I had at the law firm; I would get to support young people in the very way that would have helped me when I was a student; I would get to do work that made a difference, supporting thousands of students who would go on to do so many amazing things with their lives; and I would get to create a lasting legacy at a two-hundred-year-old institution.

The trade-offs: I would have to drive forty-five minutes each way to work every day, and I would have to take a 50% pay cut and work in an industry I'd never worked in before. There would certainly be a learning curve. I'd have to build a positive reputation and credibility with my colleagues and counterparts in the industry, and I would have to foster and create new, supportive relationships to do my job well.

After carefully weighing the positives and negatives, I decided to take the job. I negotiated an eleven-month contract, which gave me more freedom to travel and have downtime, which made the sting of earning less money a little more bearable.

YOU ARE MORE THAN A TITLE

Reinvention can feel vulnerable. It means realizing that you are more than a position, title, profession, or company. Many of us, women especially, believe worth and identity are tied to our roles. We are so much more than that.

> Don't allow your limited vision to keep you from your purpose.

We are our skills, talents, character, experience, and all the other qualities that make us unique and special. Those attributes can be applied to many different roles. Don't allow your limited vision to keep you from your purpose.

Many professionals get stuck at a company or in a career out of fear that they won't be successful without the branding and backing of their company and title. Others get stuck in a profession because they don't see their skills as transferable. The truth is reinvention is possible and can be the very thing that leads you to your purpose. That was certainly true for me.

After a few years at Miami, as much as I enjoyed the work I was doing building and running an impactful and successful program supporting students pursuing their dream of attending law school, I began to consider what might be next for me. Yes, the work was fulfilling, the experience was so rewarding personally, and I felt like I was building something I was proud of and making a positive impact, but I got the feeling there might be something more, something different I needed to do. To be clear, you can do great, fulfilling work that is meaningful while you are on your purpose journey.

Though I was working in Miami, I lived in Cincinnati. I started noticing there were things happening in my city that I didn't love and I thought needed to change. At first, I would make a mental note and file it away. Then I started talking to people, asking what they thought about how things were going.

After a while, these thoughts became louder and more persistent. As the thoughts and ideas became louder and more persistent, I began to think about what needed to change.

Around the same time, a political leader I respected was in the process of re-entering politics. I asked her to meet for coffee. I shared how frustrated I was about what was happening in the city and that I thought our city leaders needed to get on the same page, take advantage of the opportunities available, and really work to make our city better.

She invited me to serve on the committee for the study she was working on about why women don't run for office. I agreed. One day, she invited me to join one of the focus groups because one of the women in the study couldn't participate. I hesitated initially.

I thought it was a conflict of interest for me to be on the steering committee and a participant. But she soon persuaded me. What I didn't know at the time was that this was all a setup. I answered the questions frankly and honestly.

- "No, I wouldn't consider a career in politics, because politicians are dishonest and unethical."
- "Yes, I certainly felt qualified to serve as an elected leader."
- "I had no time or family commitments that made it difficult to serve."

- "I didn't believe that politicians could really make a difference in the community; they were either too self-interested or outside interests were too powerful to allow real change."

After I completed the focus group interviews, she asked me if I wanted to run for office. I quickly responded, "No," and shared my reasons with her. I didn't want to be a politician. Absolutely not! She then asked me if I'd be willing to help her with her campaign for re-election. I hesitated at first but later agreed.

NEVER SAY NEVER

Over the course of the next year, I worked as a member of the campaign team, focused mostly on organizing house parties with her supporters to raise money, additional supporters, and awareness about her vision and plan for the city. I did not like campaigning. It felt transactional and far removed from the actual work of serving.

She won that election and asked me again whether I would consider running for public office myself. I again refused. There was no way I was going to subject myself to the tedious work of raising money, the long days and nights crisscrossing the city for event after event, listening to people constantly complain more about trash, potholes, and taxes, and less about the big, systemic issues I was passionate about.

I continued to build the prelaw program at Miami and put the idea of running for office behind me. Or so I thought. The experience of working on that campaign opened my eyes. I began to see the challenges in my city more clearly, they became more personal, and I started believing I could help solve them.

Even as I was doing great and important work with students in Oxford, I couldn't help but think, perhaps, I could make an even bigger difference if I could use my gifts and talents to help more people. A natural-born problem-solver and self-proclaimed world changer, I began to convince myself my type of leadership was needed and I had a duty to step up and help in any way I could.

On the path to purpose, there are "lightbulb" moments—when your vision becomes so clear you realize you must take the next step. Eventually, I called that political leader and invited her for breakfast. She agreed to meet with me, and as soon as we sat down, she looked me directly in the eyes and said, "You're going to do it, aren't you?" She knew what I was thinking and the reason I'd asked to meet.

I replied, "Yes, I'm going to do it." Saying yes in that moment took me on a totally different course, one that has led me even to my work today.

As we learned from the study, there is tremendous power in asking someone to do something. The number one reason women don't run for office is simple: no one asked them to run. When asked, women are more likely to run. I would guess this is true for many professions and leadership in general. There is also power in saying "yes."

> On the path to purpose, there are "lightbulb" moments— when your vision becomes so clear you realize you must take the next step.

When counseling prelaw students at Miami University, I challenged them to say "yes" to every request that was made of them. Of course, that doesn't include things that are illegal or unethical. But if someone asked them to volunteer for an organization, attend an event, or take on a leadership role or a significant responsibility, they should say yes.

For three months, just say yes. When I was in college, I said "yes" to everything. If we haven't already established it, I have always been a busybody with a really bad case of FOMO. Saying yes to everything for my entire life has led me down some amazing paths and opened doors I never imagined, but it also led to overwork and burnout.

I want to put a pin in our conversation here to emphasize the importance of balance and intention, which we will cover a little more later.

But a lot of students I counseled had the exact opposite problem. They rejected nearly every offer presented to them and missed the chance to learn, network, to build their skills and their resume, all things that would prove important if they wanted to attend law school and advance in their careers. So, when I challenged them to "say yes," they realized there were a lot of opportunities they needed and really loved that they would have missed had they not said "yes." Many of them, after my initial challenge, even began seeking more opportunities to lead and grow.

Once I decided to run for office, I was on my way to another stage in my reinvention journey, my fourth shift since I began my post-college career. Marketing, which was my first job post-college before law school, law, academia, and now politics. Four jobs and four different industries.

Reinvention, for me, had many benefits. I learned so much from each of my experiences, and I was able to transfer many of those skills to the next career. At each stage of my journey, I gained friends and colleagues, people who have supported me in later transitions. I became more resilient and less sensitive to change. In fact, I have learned to embrace and appreciate change.

I learned to connect with people and to master new ways of doing things very quickly, to simplify and synthesize, to get from zero to one hundred very quickly. My learning curve has gotten less steep with every career transition I have made. In my five years at Miami, I learned to navigate the academic world. I gained so much knowledge about teaching, counseling, developing programs, and leadership, all skills I still use in my work. I made many allies and colleagues in the field, many of whom remain a part of my inner circle to this day.

I decided to stay in my role at Miami University while I ran for public office; I still had work to complete there, and I wasn't guaranteed to win—in fact, it was rare for a candidate to win an election for Cincinnati City Council on the first try. Remember what I said earlier about playing all sides to the middle and having a Plan B? I wasn't ready to give up my role at Miami University and had hoped I might find a way to do both jobs IF I happened to win the election the following year.

After I launched my campaign for city council, I realized quickly that running your own campaign is very different than volunteering for someone else's. I was able to pick my team, develop my own agenda, and engage people the way I wanted. I had to learn a lot within a short window of time, and I had to trust myself to make decisions only I could make and that could greatly impact my future, either positively or negatively.

Fortunately, my previous work experiences had prepared me for most of what I encountered. My experience of overcoming obstacles as a child made me strong, determined, and fearless, all of which served me well in my first run for office.

To be clear, I am not saying it was easy. It wasn't. After about eighteen months of planning, working hard, crisscrossing the city, and talking to thousands of residents, I defied the odds and won my very first race for Cincinnati City Council. I served in that role for six years, passing legislation and building programs to combat childhood poverty, racial injustice, and human trafficking. That season was one of the most fulfilling and impactful of my life.

When I started serving on the council, I realized I had to level up quickly. I was immediately thankful for my experience at Miami, which taught me how to build programs from the ground up. In public service, after being sworn in, I moved into a new office, hired staff, and began legislating, serving, and leading. We delivered a budget less than two months after our first day of work. There was so much about that work that was so natural to me. There were also so many parts of the work that were unfamiliar, almost like learning a new language and a new culture. Adaptability is a key part of reinvention.

> Adaptability is a key part of reinvention.

Not everyone has to leave their job or career to fulfill their purpose. Reinvention doesn't require you to leave your company, either. You can pursue purpose and reinvent yourself right where you are.

PROFILES IN PURPOSE & REINVENTION

In my work with executive leaders pursuing purpose, change is often the great inhibitor. It can be tough to envision shifting from your present circumstances to a new way of doing things. I want to highlight two amazing leaders I supported through the decision-making process as they contemplated making the shift. Their stories illustrate some of the demands, both internally and externally, leaders face when considering shifting from making a living to making a legacy.

KIMBERLY "THE SIDE HUSTLER"

The first leader, Kimberly, was a senior level manager at a Fortune 500 company. She had over twelve years of experience in her industry and eight years in her company, and throughout her career she had taken on more and more senior levels of responsibility. She had proven herself an essential member of the team and was looking to either take the next step in her company or branch out and start her own business.

Personally, she was a mother and the breadwinner in her household. She was financially secure and had even begun to take on freelance work in her field. But the prospect of leaving her company and starting her own business was scary, in part because she was not yet prepared to replace her salary, and she worried that if her small business couldn't support her she would be financially strapped. She and I met and discussed her situation.

First, as I do with all leaders I advise, I asked her what she really wanted. I asked questions like, "What is your passion?" "What do you dream of doing?" She expressed she really loved her work. So we didn't have a situation where career reinvention was required. She also really liked her job but struggled with her reporting structure and felt she wasn't being valued.

This is a concern I hear a lot from leaders, especially those in large companies where there are layers and layers of leadership, often far too much oversight and control, and typically a gatekeeper who filters responsibilities, workload, and assignments. When leaders get to a certain level, particularly if they have done their job for a long time and have become experts at that job, it's not uncommon for them to hit the wall and begin to look up. It's at that stage they begin looking for greater responsibility and autonomy, more creative freedom and control, and the ability to use their gifts and talents in a more significant way in the organization.

In larger, more complex organizations, there might not be a natural place for that energy to be directed, particularly if their direct supervisor hoards responsibility. I see this in so many instances with leaders who are looking to make a shift. In those instances, it's not always the right call to leave the organization. It's really important to determine the source of your frustration at work before making a move.

It Starts with You

Ask yourself, what is really driving my unhappiness at work? If you make a move to another organization without answering that question, you may jump out of the frying pan and into the skillet. You may leave your organization and transition to another one and find yourself in the same situation. Whenever you begin to feel like it's time to make a change, transition, or shift at work or at home, or in your civic or community life, ask yourself two questions:

1. What about you needs to change?
2. What circumstances around you need to change to make the situation better?

In nearly every situation, something about you needs to change. I've found that "changing you" first can provide the clarity you need to figure out what else needs to change. It always starts with you. Once you've changed the things you need to change, you can more clearly see the things that need to change around you.

In Kimberly's situation, in some ways, she had enabled the work environment she was in because she had never expressed the things that caused her stress and unhappiness. The source of her stress and unhappiness was wanting more freedom and control over her work. She wanted to see the promotion path: what did her next ten years in the organization look like? What steps was the organization prepared to take to invest in her future leadership?

She wanted more ownership over her work, she wanted more responsibility, and she wanted to know her company was prepared to walk her up the leadership ladder as far as she was able to climb. She'd never said those things to her supervisor. She'd never shared that with her mentors and trusted advisers in the organization. Instead, she'd accepted the work she was given and did the work proficiently, never demanding more.

I've learned this mistake is not uncommon. So many leaders believe supervisors instinctively know what we want and desire, even if we haven't expressed it. Some of us worry that if we express dissatisfaction with our current work situation, we will be seen as ungrateful and will be ignored or punished for speaking up and telling the truth. So we remain silent, keeping our feelings to ourselves until we hit the ceiling of frustration and leave the organization.

The challenge with that response is, in this scenario, you haven't changed the thing you need to change—when you head to another organization, you will find yourself in the same scenario. Hence, jumping from the frying pan into the skillet.

Freedom Is Priceless

Kimberly realized she needed to express her interest to her supervisor. But there was more to Kimberly's story. In the freelance work she was doing, she really loved that she was paid well and able to control her work. She was being paid more to do the same work as her full-time job and had the ability to decide which projects she accepted and how she executed the work. Freedom.

Often when people want to make shifts in their work environment, freedom is a major consideration. Having control over what and how you do a job is a major factor for people when deciding to become entrepreneurs. Realizing the real value of your work in the marketplace is another.

Kimberly had realized she could experience more freedom and make more money by starting her own business. The challenge was she wasn't ready, personally, or financially to take the leap. We needed to buy her more time. She needed to find a way to create more space at work while she worked her plan to make her side business her full-time gig.

There are a lot of people who work full time and have a side hustle, working their job and saving money until they feel secure enough to leave their job and hang their own shingle. Because Kimberly wasn't 100% sure that her employer would respond positively to her request for more freedom and responsibility, we discussed the possibility of a lateral move to another company. Or perhaps a lateral move within her company to a different department with a different supervisor.

The Power of a Plan

Meanwhile we worked through her business plan. How long would it take for her to save up and build enough business in her freelance work to go into business for herself full-time? We did the math together and realized that conservatively, it would take about five years. She could take on more outside projects and hire contractors to do the work while she continued to work full-time at her company, earning the salary and benefits she needed to take care of her family.

She would earn a percentage of her contractors' time, which she would add to her savings, while building a clientele that could support her and others in the future. Once she had enough contracts to more than support herself and others, she would make her exit. In the meantime, we needed a plan to keep herself happy at work. She explored other companies to see if there might be opportunities to advance somewhere else and sought out lateral positions within the company. She expressed an interest in more responsibility in her reporting structure within her department as well.

This is what I call playing all sides to the middle. In college, when I was applying for law school, I also applied for jobs, *just in case.* There is something about growing up poor that creates a strong need for security and always having a Plan B. It can be a blessing and a curse. After speaking with her supervisor, she understood she would not have the support in her current department to take on more and grow as a leader.

She made a lateral move within her company that allowed her that freedom. For the next five years or maybe fewer, she will work at her current job and build her business, doing freelance work, until she is ready to make her exit.

LISA "THE UNSUNG HERO"

Another leader I work with had the opposite problem. Lisa was given too much responsibility and not enough support to get all the work done. She was overworked, under-appreciated, under-resourced, and just plain over it.

When she came to me for help, she was ready to leave her company. She pretty much had one foot out the door. I challenged her a bit on this. I asked her to put together a list of the things she loved about her job and a list of the things she would need to stay. As you can imagine, that's the last thing she wanted to do considering she was fed up and had made up her mind she was leaving.

Based on her reputation and experience, leaving would have been an easy thing to do. Because of this, I realized I had better work quickly if I was going to coach her to truly consider what would be the best alternative for her long-term. If you love your company and you love what you do, leaving that company is a risk. You could find yourself in a new company and realize too late that you miss what you had. That's the 80-20 rule. It is important, before making a shift, to understand your motivation.

What is really driving your desire for change? If you leave a wonderful situation where you have 80% of what you need and 20% of what you hate, you could end up in a place that has the 20% of what you were looking for and little to none of the great things you left behind. Instead, I coach leaders to first negotiate for as much of the 20%

of what you need in your current job, and then if you don't get it, use your leverage when seeking a new role to get 100% of what you need before you transition.

You have far more leverage when you are looking for a job than after you've accepted the offer. You may not get 100% in your new role—just make sure you get at least what you currently have and then some. If not, then you're jumping out of the frying pan and into the fire, into a worse situation because of the pain and struggle it takes to start over and the risk that comes with leaving something you love and it not working out.

I want to be clear, as someone who has reinvented herself many times, I am not opposed to risk taking, and I recognize there are times when you must go. Every step in the purpose journey is worthwhile because we learn so much from each experience we have. But it's important to take the time and carefully consider why you are leaving and mitigate the risk by asking the questions needed to ensure you end up in a better situation than the one you're leaving.

When Lisa shared her list with me, it was clear that she loved her work and she was fulfilling her purpose at work. She had been with her organization for twenty years and had gained an excellent reputation. She was great at her job, she worked hard, and she was a respected leader at her company and in her industry.

Leaders like Lisa are the unsung heroes who shoulder more and more responsibility and work, and to show their "appreciation" the company gives them more work, but not necessarily the pay they deserve and rarely a promotion. So often leaders like Lisa work for people who should report to them. They do their boss's job and make them look good, and they get overlooked during bonus and promotion time. It's easy to get frustrated in that situation.

But as Kimberly learned, it's important to do the work of determining **what you need to change and what needs to change around you.**

If You Don't A-S-K, You Won't G-E-T

If you're in a situation like Lisa's, ask yourself a few questions: 1) in what ways have I enabled the situation I inherited? 2) if I was in a new organization, would I do the same thing? 3) have I asked for/demanded the things I need from my employer?

Like Kimberly, Lisa had not yet asked—or demanded—more from her supervisor. A high achiever, when things aren't done well, she takes them on to make sure they are done perfectly. She would ask for help, but then when asked to take on something more she wouldn't refuse it for lack of time or support.

Instead she would take on more and do it exceptionally well, on time, as expected. She was asking for more support but never showed that she needed it. Inside, she was silently suffering from burnout.

She didn't feel comfortable not taking on new tasks or whatever was needed to get the job done, and she wasn't willing to sacrifice quality, so we worked herself even harder to get more done. Catch-22. She was exhausted and she was done. In the rare instance where she requested more help, she was promised it, but when she didn't get it she didn't challenge it; she kept working. Her supervisor found squeakier wheels that took priority.

Because Lisa was already preparing to leave, I convinced her she had nothing to lose in going to her company and asking for everything she wanted and needed. The worst they could do is say "No," and since she was marketable and in demand she could walk right out and go somewhere else with no problem.

But if she was able to use her excellent work and reputation as leverage in a new company, she could do the same with her current company. I advised her to put everything into her list of demands, plus the kitchen sink, all on the table. We worked together on a list because, in my experience, I've seen that selfless, committed leaders like Lisa rarely ask for enough. She laughed as we put the list together because she was convinced she'd never get it, and it felt silly for her to ask.

But I reminded her that we were creating the perfect scenario for her to stay. If they said "No" to something, she could then decide whether it was worth it to stay or leave. But if she didn't ask for everything, she risked not having everything she needed if she stayed or, worse, leaving without giving herself the chance to have everything she wanted at a workplace she genuinely loved.

Lisa had leverage because she was already working herself ragged at her company, she had very little risk because she was in demand and was highly likely to be hired by another company, and she had a spouse who was sharing the financial burden with her. That gave her cover, a security blanket, in case she left her current job and didn't find a new one right away. It's important to consider all these things when considering making a move because not everyone has the same very real and practical constraints when leaving their job.

Remember that Kimberly needed to move laterally before she could move out because her life and work situations were different. If that is your situation, follow Kimberly's path and create a longer-term exit strategy. As I've said before, I don't advise blowing up your life to pursue your purpose. Risk is a part of any journey, especially this one, but taking calculated risk is more sustainable. It's a marathon, not a sprint, remember?

After we made the list, Lisa went to her boss with her demands. She was strong and confident in making her case for more money, more support, more time off, and a promotion. Not long after she met with her employer, they returned with their answer. She got everything she wanted! The lesson from Lisa's example is one of my favorite ones: "If you don't ASK, you won't GET."

Asking for what you need, whether in your work life or your personal life is key to getting it. So often we assume the person in our lives knows what we want or need or even cares enough to give it to us without a demand. "Power concedes nothing without a demand." If you want your circumstances to change, it starts with changing you then demanding things change around you.

The examples of Kimberly and Lisa are illustrative of two major issues I see when helping leaders shift from making a living to making a legacy. First, **it starts with you.** Most leaders haven't done the deep, real, and difficult work of understanding the things they need to change internally.

Self-reflection and self-awareness are key to understanding your motivation and what drives you. When we fail to do that self-reflection, we repeat the same patterns and end up with the same results. Shifting to a new role without changing yourself won't change your outcome. It's like complaining that your feet are tired and worn out from wearing a pair of uncomfortable high-heeled shoes that are a size too small, only to buy another expensive pair of heels in the same size. They may look different, but they are still gonna hurt, just in new ways.

> If you want your circumstances to change, it starts with changing you then demanding things change around you.

Second, **figure out the things that need to change around you.** Take stock of the things in your workplace, your family life, your civic and community work that aren't serving you, and work to negotiate or change those things before making a move. Often, when people shift from role to role searching for a good fit or to be fulfilled, they carry old baggage with them and don't realize they haven't resolved the issues that caused them to move in the first place.

I made the same mistakes in my early work transitions. I blamed the work, my boss, my clients, coworkers, and my assignments for my lack of fulfillment. "It's just not a good fit," I said. The truth is I hadn't figured out what I needed or wanted, and my organization couldn't give me something I didn't know to ask for. It would take me a little while to figure out what I really wanted to do and be and the type of support I needed to be successful.

Once I learned that, I had to learn to express those needs to my employer and request, negotiate, or demand those things I needed to stay there. Or, if they were unable to provide what I needed, to have the courage to leave for a place that could. And as we learned from both Kimberly and Lisa, if you are considering leaving your current company or career, make sure the place you transition to can provide all the things you couldn't get from your current company.

THE ABCS OF PURPOSE AND REINVENTION

This journey of purpose and reinvention requires three things from you. These are critical steps you must follow, parts of yourself you must confront, challenge, and transform for this journey to be one that is impactful and lasting. I call them the ABCs: authenticity, breakthrough, and change. Let's take a moment—deep breath here—to walk through each one together.

AUTHENTICITY

Authenticity is about knowing yourself and accepting yourself for who you are, flaws and all. It's about realizing the unique person you are is exactly what the world needs. It's about valuing the contributions you make to the world, especially when you are most yourself. It's about realizing you are valuable, as you are, not because of what you do.

Love Has Everything to Do with It

When I speak to audiences across the country, especially women, I ask them the same question. Do you love yourself for who you are right now? Not if you were skinnier, could dance like Beyoncè, or if you had more money. But you, as you are, right now? I ask them to raise their hands if they love themselves as they are right then.

Whether I am in a room full of accomplished high school girls or executive women, the response is the same. Without fail, in a room of one hundred women, I might see one or two raised hands. How would you answer that question? It surprises me every time that more hands aren't raised, and no matter the audience, young or old, novice or seasoned, the vast majority of women I speak with don't love themselves. I rarely see this with men, who tend to be overly confident and content with who they are and how they show up, despite their very real flaws and challenges.

I am on a mission to show more women how to love themselves so they can lead more authentic lives. Love and authenticity are essential partners; they are connected in a codependent relationship. One requires the other to be successful. If you don't love yourself, you won't exist authentically.

By the same token, if you don't know who you are and don't lead an authentic existence, you won't ever love yourself—at least not the real you. I am heartened by the Howard Thurman quote, "Come Alive," which is the title to one of my keynote speeches. Howard Thurman said, "Don't ask what the world needs. Ask yourself what makes you come alive and go do that. Because what the world needs is more people who come alive."

Such a powerful inspiration and the opposite of what we are taught to believe. So often we try to shape-shift or mold ourselves into someone or something we think is needed, something we think would make other people happy, or make us appear prestigious, honorable, or popular.

The truth is everyone has a purpose. And when you are operating in your purpose, you are your most true and authentic self. There are people who need you to be the person you were meant to be because they are going to be served by you fulfilling your purpose. And if you aren't there because you are doing something else, then they won't get what they need from you to do the thing they need to do in this world. By the same token, if you aren't operating in your purpose, you won't get what you need either.

There are four steps to living more authentically. I call them the four S's: See, Speak, Stand, and Shine. These are four relatively simple concepts that will ultimately help us better understand, become, and appreciate who we truly are.

See

See is about how we view ourselves, alone and in relation to the world around us. How we see ourselves shapes so much about how we navigate the world. It starts early. Some of it is intrinsic, a part of our nature, but there is a large part of our self-image that is influenced by society, our family, our friends, the people in our inner circle and people who come into our lives at different stages.

To be clear, we are who we are, fundamentally. We also evolve over time. Our physical appearance changes and so does our perspective and our character. We can also do things that change us both externally and internally, specifically our physical appearance and self-perception.

I barely recognize myself after being pampered by the hair and makeup glam team at ABC News. I walk a little straighter, even strut a little when I've got a full face of makeup, gorgeous butterfly lashes, when my edges have been laid and my hair is freshly straightened or my locks perfectly coifed by my stylist's gifted hands. Put me in a dress that fits just right in my power color, look out! Looking good makes me feel good. But at my core, I am who I am, regardless of how I appear.

When I accomplish a goal or do something great, I feel taller and walk proud like a peacock. After I film a pitch-perfect segment on TV, receive an award for work I've done for the community, or when one of my candidates wins a hard-fought race with my support and guidance, I blow kisses at myself in the mirror, give myself a wink, and tell myself I am wonderful—and I believe it in that moment.

That sense of accomplishment makes me feel six feet tall, even though I stand at a solid 5 foot 3 ¾ inches on any other day. When we look good and feel good, it changes how we see ourselves, but we are fundamentally the same. In contrast, what about the days when we are walking around sick, tired, pale, battered, and feeling like a mere shadow of ourselves? We feel like less than who we are, smaller and less significant.

What about when we suffer a major loss, when we don't hit the mark, or catastrophe strikes, and we feel helpless to respond to it? We can't seem to find our rhythm, our footing, can't even pick ourselves off the floor.

When George Floyd was murdered back in 2021, I sat on the floor of my bedroom crying for three solid days, unable to move, broken and defeated. I felt like the work that I had dedicated myself to was in vain, feeling helpless and hopeless in my own skin, my value, my self-worth as a black person diminished and I was being reduced to less than fully human. I felt worthless and useless in those moments.

But who I was intrinsically hadn't changed. Yvette is still Yvette, whether walking tall or crying on the floor. When we go through difficult moments, it's important to remember what we SEE changes from day to day. But whether you look or feel great or not so great, you are still you.

Confession time. I wasn't a pretty baby—okay, to be 100% honest, I was an ugly baby. I know it's not polite or politically correct to call a baby ugly, but I have heard the stories and seen the pictures. I had rows of bags under my eyes and under my chin. Imagine Benjamin Button as a baby.

My grandmother called me an old soul, and based on my pictures, I looked like I had lived a thousand lifetimes when I was born. As I got older, I got cuter—the triple chin blended naturally into my face and the bags disappeared. I was a pretty cute toddler.

During my preteen years, I was considered smart, cute, fun, and laid back. Several years later, I "grew into" the sexy, ride-or-die chick. But I wasn't considered beautiful. I had friends and relatives who were naturally beautiful by traditional societal standards. I was not.

Let's put a pin here and digress for a moment. I was darker skinned at a time when lighter skin was considered more beautiful. I had kinky hair, which my grandmother straightened with a hot comb until she finally let me get a relaxer. I was skinny until I "filled out" during puberty, and I desperately needed braces but didn't get them until college when my dad had saved enough money to get them for me.

I didn't see myself as beautiful, and I let myself embrace the cute label because of it. It wasn't until I was much older that I started to see myself as beautiful, but those early years shaped the way I allowed myself to be treated and placed limits on the opportunities I reached for. I remember as a preteen one of my friends was recruited to be a model, back when those companies would hold open sessions for young girls to come in, do a photo shoot, and then be screened for a modeling gig.

My friend had a lighter complexion than I did and conformed more naturally to traditional standards of beauty. I asked to tag along to the appointment, hoping they would see me and give me a chance to become a model too. Well, they didn't.

According to them, I was too dark-skinned, too short, and not beautiful enough to be a model. Despite what I already "knew" to be true about myself, I was devastated when they rejected me. That news affirmed the negative perception I had about myself. In so many ways, our early experiences and encounters can shape our self-perception for a lifetime. No matter how many times someone calls me beautiful, even today, I still see myself as more "cute" than "beautiful."

This same philosophy applies to the nonphysical aspects of ourselves. I was always naturally smart, but I wasn't the smartest. I was athletic but not the fastest or the strongest. I was naturally good at certain activities but always had to work hard to be great.

I grew up believing I was not good enough, that I had to work twice as hard as everyone else, and that I was only as good as my last accomplishment. This became hard-wired in my brain, a belief I have learned to actively reject and push down. I still struggle with this, but I'm committed to seeing myself truthfully and with love.

Perhaps the most dangerous influence on our self-perception is our tendency to compare ourselves to others. We live in a world where we are constantly bombarded by standards and symbols of beauty, success, wealth, and happiness.

When I ask someone how they see themselves, they almost always compare themselves to someone else. *I'm not as talented as Beyoncè or as beautiful as Halle Berry. I wish I was as fit as Angela Bassett or had Jennifer Aniston's natural radiance.* This type of thinking is harmful because we can't be someone else. It's impossible. Even if we could, we shouldn't try to be anyone other than ourselves.

When we do that, it erodes the unique value we hold and diminishes those parts of us no one else possesses. Comparing yourself to others creates an unrealistic standard you just can't meet. Being your best self is tough enough.

I know we can be conditioned to believe we are "less than," and that can be hard to overcome, even though we know these are only beliefs that are not real but instead internal and external forces shape how we see ourselves. Thankfully, there are ways to counteract these forces.

Speak

The second "S" is for "speak." Words are powerful. The words we speak shape how we see ourselves and ultimately who we become. So often, we allow others' words to influence how we see ourselves. For instance, the limitations we place on ourselves are often based more on what someone said we couldn't do or be, which we internalize and believe to be true. Those words can become an invisible fence around us, keeping us from our greatness, our full potential.

The key to unlocking that fence is speaking words of affirmation to ourselves, telling ourselves the things that are true about us. I think about the scarecrow in the movie *The Wiz*. He spends years hanging in a field telling himself he doesn't have a brain, he isn't smart, and there are scarecrows around him reinforcing that negative message.

The thing he believes about himself isn't actually true. With Dorothy, he sets off to find the wizard, who he believes can give him what he thinks he lacks. In the end, he realizes he had a brain all along—he was already smart. He just needed to believe it. Once he could see what was already true about himself, it changed his outlook and his life for the better. So many of us are like that scarecrow.

We don't realize how smart, powerful, bold, and capable we are. We may even attract people who reaffirm the very feelings of insecurity within us. But when we can identify and speak truth about ourselves, we unlock our power to be our truest, most authentic selves, which leads us on our path toward our purpose.

Affirmation isn't about ego, it isn't about hyping yourself up, and it certainly isn't about convincing yourself you are something you are not. In fact, it's quite the opposite. Speaking positive words of truth about ourselves helps us develop a broader and better understanding of who we are, often the part of us we hide from the world, and from ourselves.

If you don't already engage in an affirmation practice, I encourage you to create affirmations that are actually true about you, perhaps words that are unique to you. When I work with groups of women leaders, I begin by reciting words from one of my favorite songs "Beautiful Flower" by India Arie, phrases which also happen to be characteristically true about leaders: beauty, resilience, and strength, are qualities in women leaders that should be acknowledged and celebrated.

Next, I encourage leaders to think about words or phrases that are their own, that are true for them. Saying affirmative words counteracts the untrue, negative words we hear about ourselves. Often these words are stereotypes or words that have been used to limit or oppress people. For instance, women are often characterized as "powerless," so when a woman refers to herself as "powerful," it counteracts a false, long-held belief, one she has likely been told repeatedly.

For me, even though I was intelligent and hard-working, as a black woman, I've felt I had to overcome stereotyping to prove I am smart and capable. To counteract that insecurity, I sometimes affirm: "I am brilliant. I am capable. I am a genius." When I say those words, my spirit lifts, and over time, those words come alive inside me, and I start to believe them. Those words become armor against the weapons of criticism and limited expectations I encounter.

From Affirmation to Aspirational

There is an arc from affirmation to the aspirational; there is something powerful about speaking words that represent the things you want to see in your life in the future. But they are different words that mean different things, particularly when the affirmation is for us. To "affirm" means to "state as fact; assert strongly and publicly." The word "aspire" means to "direct one's hopes or ambitions toward achieving something."

Simply put, affirmation is about what we are or our present truth, and aspiration is about what we hope to be, perhaps our future truth. In this section, I want to distinguish between the two. Affirmation is firmly rooted in authenticity because it is about acknowledging, celebrating, and honoring who we are today. I think about the words Abilene spoke over the young girl, Mae, in the movie, *The Help.*

She is helping Mae not only see what is true, that she is intelligent, compassionate, and significant, but also what is possible for her. In many ways, Abilene is affirming Mae, giving support and encouragement, while at the same time affirming herself by stating things that are also true about her, and these are things that neither of them can see. She's counteracting false, negative words that have been attributed to them.

Aspiration can be valuable because we often don't see our own potential, and when we speak about our hopes and dreams, we give ourselves permission to walk forward into our destiny.

When I was a little girl and said, "I'm going to be a lawyer," I was harnessing the power of aspiration. The words were what I both desired and believed to be true for me, even though I hadn't lived them yet. Saying them aloud made them real for me, which helped me see them as possible. My words held power.

Truth Is Your Superpower

Speaking truth is key to authenticity. For instance, if you are not naturally patient, saying, "I am patient" isn't rooted in authenticity, and it's important to acknowledge that in the present. Living life on purpose is about each of us treating our unique gifts as valuable, because you are valuable, just the way you are. Patience is a virtue, for sure, but it's not innate for some people. I fall squarely in the impatient category, for what it's worth.

> Living life on purpose is about each of us treating our unique gifts as valuable, because you are valuable, just the way you are.

Remember that authenticity is about seeing yourself as you are, seeing those characteristics and traits as essential and important to you and the world, and speaking the truth to yourself so you love the unique parts of yourself and the value you, as you are, bring to the world. It's not about being something you are not. That would be inauthentic or dishonest. It may also be an exercise in futility or perhaps better suited for a book about change management.

This affirmation exercise is about authenticity, recognizing and appreciating yourself for who you truly are, and speaking those truths about you to reinforce who you are. For instance, as someone who is not very patient, I would not affirm that "I am patient" but instead choose something else that is true for me. I might say, "I am driven, I know what I want, and I'm working diligently to achieve it." My impatience, my drive, and persistence have served me and my work in the world in so many ways. So my impatience is valuable.

Take some time later today and write down words that are true about you and practice saying those words to yourself. Not only will you feel great about who you are, those words may reveal something important about your purpose you hadn't considered. Remember, the world needs you, as you are today, whole, happy, and at your best. Speaking positive words of truth about yourself is essential to being your most authentic self.

WORDS OF AFFIRMATION

_____

_____

_____

_____

_____

_____

_____

_____

_____

_____

_____

_____

_____

_____

_____

_____

_____

_____

_____

Stand

The third "S" is for "stand." A key part of pursuing purpose is being at the place you are meant to be at the right time. I love the quote, "When you determine your purpose, the universe will conspire to make it come to pass." Powerful, right?

When I hear this quote, I imagine someone attempting to walk in one direction when they are suddenly pulled back, like with a lasso, in the opposite direction and placed in the very spot where they belong. In a world where we are taught to believe either things just happen to us and we have no control over them, or we need to work hard to make things happen, this idea that the universe conspires to make things happen doesn't really fit.

But there is something very real about being clear about the things you want and are meant to do and being led to them. Some people call it manifesting, while others consider it a natural extension of intention. The truth is we spend a lot of time figuring out where we are supposed to be and can get distracted by the demands of life and very realistic constraints on our time, capacity, and ability.

You may have dreamed long ago that you wanted to be a teacher, but someone told you teachers don't get paid much, so you decided to pursue a career in business so you could make a good living. You dreamed about being a doctor but didn't have the years or the resources to devote to medical school. You dreamed about starting your own business, but you needed health insurance and a steady paycheck to take care of your family.

So many of us have made trade-offs in our lives and wound up somewhere so far away from the place we thought we should be, perhaps the place we wanted to be. Then you wake up one day, perhaps financially secure but feeling disconnected from your work. You have stability, but you don't feel motivated by your current job or career.

To be clear, these are very real considerations we each must make every day. But remember, you have the power to make different choices. You can decide you want to make a change and live a life filled with purpose.

You can choose purpose over a paycheck, legacy over prestige, impact over fame.

Many people wait until later in their career, or when tragedy or catastrophe strikes to choose to be in the place they are meant to be, doing the work they are supposed to be doing. A once-in-a-generation pandemic has caused so many people to make the very same choice.

As I shared earlier, when I decided to leave the law firm in search of my purpose, I made a few trade-offs: less money, less stability, and security. But I knew the work I was doing wasn't what I was ultimately supposed to be doing. I knew there was something different, something more for me out there. I was never going to get there if I didn't take the first step to determine and declare my purpose. Once I did, the universe conspired. And it moved me to places and situations I would have never considered or dreamed about.

Just Do It

The deeper lesson, one I reinforce for the leaders I advise, is to "just do it." Don't fight the feeling you get, and don't miss the very real opportunities that come your way that are designed to get you closer to your purpose. I don't regret the course of my life and career. I know it all worked out for me, and each experience taught me the lessons and the skills I needed for the one down the road.

For instance, in pursuit of my dream of becoming a lawyer, I got my undergraduate degrees in mass communications (electronic journalism and radio, television, and film production) and political science. Today, I serve as a political strategist and television commentator. I also served as an elected leader.

When I pursued those college degrees, I didn't know my career path would perfectly meld those two areas. I pursued a political science degree because most students considering law school followed that, plus ... I wanted to be Oprah Winfrey. The universe conspired. During my years as a public servant, I often did interviews with media, and during the mayor's race I prepared for and participated in several debates.

So when I was invited for to join the Roundtable for ABC News as a political commentator for the first time, I wasn't nervous. I felt ready. When the executive team at ABC asked me how I was so calm and confident in the chair during my first national TV appearance, I replied, "I've been preparing for this role for quite a while."

Stand on the X. Do it now. Act as though today were your last day. What things would you pursue and what things would you let go of? Think about the people who are waiting for you there, the people who need you operating in your purpose because their journey intersects yours at that moment.

What We Get When We Let Go

Perhaps you are where you belong professionally but not personally. You are fulfilling your purpose in your career and work life, but you haven't prioritized purpose at home. Maybe you are single and desire to be married but are so busy working you don't have time to invest in yourself, take time away, or date. I can relate to that scenario.

At one point in my life, I'd made a conscious choice to devote myself to work. I had a list and a timeline, and career came first. I had convinced myself I didn't need marriage or a relationship to be happy. I felt that if and when I was supposed to be in a relationship, love would find me. When I occasionally made time for dates, I was often distracted. My long laundry list of qualifications for a mate kept me from getting close to anyone or letting anyone get close to me. I was setting myself up for a life that wasn't my purpose.

Turns out, I was supposed to be married and be a bonus mom to three amazing daughters. I was able to walk into that purpose once I let the list go and got honest with myself about what I wanted and the changes I would need to make to live that life. One day, after realizing work would not ever make me complete, I abandoned the list, and I wrote a letter to God asking for what I really needed (and a few wants). It was simple. I wanted love and support. Looking back at that letter, I realize that few things from my original "list" were in the letter. Because at that point in my life, I was much clearer about what I needed. And the universe conspired. I read the letter to my husband several years after we started dating, and he said, "That sounds like me." I replied, "It IS you."

I encourage you to start manifesting the things you want, the things that are meant for you. Go through the process of determining what you really need and declare what you need to God, the universe, a best friend, a therapist, anyone you trust. As we declare, it gives the thing life and makes it real for us. And the universe will conspire to make those things happen. Like other aspects of your purpose journey, it won't happen overnight. It will be like a rollercoaster ride, and you may experience a few disappointments along the way. But it will happen.

This is true in our careers and in our personal lives and community work. No more excuses.

Shine

The fourth and final "S" is Shine. Shine your star. As leaders, we can feel insecure about applying for a promotion, overwhelmed by a new responsibility or project, or nervous when people or parameters shift in our workplace. Insecurity breeds fear and doubt, which can stop us from reaching our full potential.

Shining your star is about recognizing your very real accomplishments.

To live in your purpose, you must show up as your full self. You need to see yourself as powerful and capable. We learned earlier about how the things we say to ourselves can change our self-perception. Shining your star is about recognizing your very real accomplishments. It's about giving yourself credit for the things you do well. We often forget to take the time to celebrate our wins.

Some of us are raised to "be humble" and that acknowledging your accomplishments is bragging or boastful, which is somehow distasteful or disgraceful. I hear this often from female leaders and leaders of color. My response: if it's rooted in truth, there is no shame in celebrating it! Celebrating your accomplishments is the surest way to encourage more success. It's infectious and addictive to receive a high five or an atta girl. You shouldn't wait for someone else to do that for you, especially since we often struggle to forget our losses and failures but rarely remember our wins.

> Checking your receipts is like your best friend who reminds you of all the great things you've done in the past when you worry you can't do something big.

The best indicator of future success is past success. I encourage you to remember you can do hard things. You can overcome obstacles; you can make big things happen. You know this because of the obstacles you've overcome before, the big things you've accomplished in the past, the tough times you've navigated through to success. I call this mindset "checking your receipts."

Checking your receipts is like your best friend who reminds you of all the great things you've done in the past when you worry you can't do something big. When I was struggling to start my own business, I would occasionally forget the things I had done in the past that had prepared me for the thing I was working toward.

In those moments I would call my best friend, who fortunately has a memory like an elephant and never forgets a thing, and share my concerns with her about a big project or venture I was taking on. Without fail, she would say "Wait a minute, didn't you give a speech two years ago for a group twice the size of this one? You've done this before and completely nailed it—you've got this."

So when you nail that project your boss asked you to complete in record time, shine your star. When you land the big client your company has been courting for years, shine your star. When you get the kids in bed and dinner on the table without a cut, scrape, bruise, or visit to the emergency room, shine your star. I think you get the idea.

Once you've racked up a few wins and your star is all shined up, you will have the confidence you need to take on the next major challenge. And what are you going to do when you ace that one? That's right, you're going to shine your star again!

Checking your receipts and shining your star are important practical tools for when you are ready to step up or step out. Tracking your success and speaking confidently about your skills, abilities, and experiences are key to positive reviews or evaluations, which can lead to raises and promotions.

I often ask leaders who are getting ready to apply for a promotion to track all the great things they have done at work for three weeks to try to go back and recall all their achievements, their "shine-worthy" moments. They are always amazed at how many great things they have achieved. Then I direct them to begin a "check your receipts" practice where they record all their major achievements in the future.

When they are up for promotion, they can present, chapter and verse, all the things they have done well as evidence of their potential. Shining your star is the antidote to the coworker, supervisor, friend, or parent who constantly reminds you that you aren't good enough. It's the encouragement you need when the voices in your head tell you your success was just dumb luck and not a result of your skill, dedication, and hard work.

In my own life, I've been fortunate to have people cheer me on. As a young girl, I would run home when I got a good grade or won an award or a championship and tell my grandmother my good news with enthusiasm. She would say, "Good job, baby," and tell me she was proud of me.

I shared my dreams with her, and even though they seemed impossible she encouraged me that I could do it, and when I did she'd tell everyone who would listen.

As I got older, I began to chronicle my accomplishments. In many ways, I felt every great thing I did was for my mother, who never had the chance to accomplish the things she dreamed about because of her illness, and for my grandmother who sacrificed everything to give me the opportunity to have a good life. I shine my star for every little girl who is watching me, believing she can do what I've done and even greater things.

I celebrate my wins for every person who discouraged me because I was a little poor black girl from the projects, believing I couldn't accomplish my goals. I shine my star to counteract my tendency to overthink my mistakes and my failures. I shine my star so my future self remembers what we're made of and knows we can overcome whatever comes our way.

Living on purpose, authentically requires that you shine your star. Why? Because your accomplishments are who you are. Knowing yourself and your potential is key to fulfilling your purpose. When purpose feels beyond your reach, unattainable, and too big to accomplish, by shining your star you realize your purpose is, in fact, possible.

SHINE YOUR STAR

_____

_____

_____

_____

_____

_____

_____

_____

_____

_____

_____

_____

_____

_____

_____

_____

_____

BREAK THROUGH OLD PATTERNS AND BELIEFS

Break through Old Beliefs

The "B" in the journey of fulfilling your purpose stands for break through. If you want to live a life of purpose, you must break through old beliefs and patterns. Let's start our discussion with beliefs. For some of us, the greatest threat to our progress isn't external—it's internal.

Our thoughts, what we believe, can hold us back and keep us trapped. We don't always realize this because we have become numb to our negative self-talk. Many of the thoughts that are most harmful to us are the things we have heard said about us that we have repeated over and over so much it becomes ingrained—a song in the soundtrack we play in our heads every day.

Limiting beliefs sound like, "I can't do that," "I'm not smart enough," "I never get that right." Limiting beliefs typically start with "I can't" and include "never" and often trigger a belief that has been longstanding, maybe something that you were criticized for earlier in life, often from someone you knew, trusted, or loved. The words spoken about you have taken hold, like a record that keeps playing in your head over and over again.

> Limiting beliefs sound like, "I can't do that," "I'm not smart enough," "I never get that right."

Every time you try to make a move, do something different, or take a different path, the record plays again. Any time you fail, or things don't work out, the record plays again, reinforcing your limiting beliefs.

You Are Not an Impostor

For women especially, one of the most significant limiting beliefs we experience is impostor syndrome. The definition of impostor syndrome is: "a psychological condition characterized by persistent doubt concerning one's abilities or accomplishments accompanied by the fear of being exposed as a fraud *despite evidence of one's ongoing success."*

When experiencing impostor syndrome, even successful and powerful, capable, and accomplished women don't believe it. Have you been there? I have! I've convinced myself I've somehow fooled people into seeing or believing something that isn't true, or I might accept the fact I am capable but diminish the significance of that capability, believing it's not good enough. Others must be inflating my value—and when they figure it out, I'll be exposed as a fraud.

Michelle Obama, one of the most powerful women in the world, admitted to having impostor syndrome. Her admission freed many other women and men to acknowledge they too don't trust their greatness is real but instead believe it's a charade. In my experience, limiting beliefs like this make it tough to be authentic and love ourselves as we are. No matter how much we accomplish, we don't believe we are good enough, pretty enough, strong enough.

> The definition of impostor syndrome is: "a psychological condition characterized by persistent doubt concerning one's abilities or accomplishments accompanied by the fear of being exposed as a fraud *despite evidence of one's ongoing success."*

The antidote to this is to take control over those thoughts that don't serve them. When I coach leaders, I encourage them to notice when a limiting belief enters their minds. This often occurs late at night when sleep won't come or when they're in the shower or otherwise not occupied. I encourage them to stop, acknowledge the limiting belief, reach up, and grab it like a cloud in the sky, pull it down, confront it with an affirmative truth, and throw it away like a piece of trash.

By confronting our limiting beliefs, those unfounded fears about our abilities and potential, we face them. That helps us see the truth. Once we see the truth, it allows us to dismiss them.

My grandmother taught me a few things that have helped me turn off the noise in my head and make sure I don't allow other people's views of me to define or limit me. She would say, "Not every package that ends on your doorstep is for you. When you see a package that isn't yours, reject it, and return it to sender. What people say about you is not your business."

Wise words from a wise woman. Grandma understood we can internalize other people's view of us when their opinions are more about them than about us. She understood we need to limit the weight we place on external ideas and views.

When I was a kid and would run to her and tell her what a mean kid said to me in school—which happened a lot because I was a nerdy, poor kid in hand-me-downs—she would simply respond, "Consider the source." That was her way of reminding me not to give credence to what others have to say, especially those who don't have our best interest at heart.

Let's take a minute and put this into practice. First, what are the things you are saying about yourself? Where do those ideas originate? Often trauma and challenging life experiences are the root of our limiting beliefs. Is there trauma in your life that you haven't resolved? Are there mistakes or failures in your past that you are bringing into your present and future?

> "Not every package that ends on your doorstep is for you. When you see a package that isn't yours, reject it, and return it to sender. What people say about you is not your business."

In addition to blocking negative messages from the outside— not accepting packages that aren't meant for you—you must replace negative beliefs with positive beliefs that are true for you. Telling yourself you are capable and recalling specific times when you demonstrated your capability (i.e., checking your receipts) will help you break through old beliefs.

Replacing "I can't" with "I can" and "I will" is another way to break through old beliefs. Words have power, especially when we control them. When I was working out to lose a few pounds right before my wedding, I wore a tank top that read "I Can, I Will" to remind me I could move my body, I could meet my goal. I got lots of compliments on that shirt, and I would often meet someone's eyes in the studio mirrors who was admiring my shirt. I got a lot of thumbs up and encouraging nods.

My words weren't just motivating me; they were motivating the people around me and then motivating me all over again. Like a boomerang. Words carry energy that can be shared and recycled. So rather than spending time recycling negative words and beliefs about yourself, put positive, affirming words in the universe instead.

In your alone time, avoid the depleting energy of going through every mistake you made, every tough conversation, every bad situation, and instead spend time reliving the great things that happened, the positive seeds you planted, and the ways your mere presence was important to someone. Let those thoughts marinate before you go to sleep at the end of a long day. Let those thoughts wake you up in the morning, wash over you in the shower, and fill your cup of coffee as you start your day.

> Rather than spending time recycling negative words and beliefs about yourself, put positive, affirming words in the universe instead.

Engaging in self-care and self-love throughout the day can combat the negative messages that will certainly come from outside forces.

Break through Old Patterns

When you are on the purpose journey, you must commit to doing things differently.

It starts with mindset, the thoughts and words we allow to occupy the space between our ears and extends to our habit and behaviors. There's so much truth in the saying, "Our thoughts become our words, our words become actions, our actions become habits, and habits become our character." The trick is often we don't notice the patterns in our behaviors. They have become a part of us, and they can leave us stuck in the same place if we don't recognize them.

The Tree Experience

A trusted adviser once counseled me on how to identify and change old patterns. He called it the tree experience.

He told me to imagine I am walking alone in the forest. After walking for quite some time, I notice a very unique tree, not like the others. It's got a wide, winding base and long, drooping branches, low enough that you can climb in the tree and have a seat. I keep walking, seeking the exit of the forest.

After walking for a good amount of time, I see the same tree again. "Huh, I've seen that tree before. It looks familiar, but that can't be the same tree. I saw it more than an hour ago." Tired, confused, and frustrated, I keep walking. After another hour of wandering, I still haven't reached the edge of the forest. "I must be lost," I say to myself. I start to get discouraged and wonder if I will ever find my way out of this forest.

I keep walking another ten minutes or so and see that tree again.

Now I'm thinking, there is no way there are three identical trees in this forest. I stop and scratch my head. I look ahead and behind me, then do a 360-degree turn in the forest. Suddenly, I realize the truth. I'd been walking in a circle.

When you are wandering through the proverbial forest and you see a tree you recognize, make note of it. If you see that tree again, it's because you're walking in a circle. Once you realize you're not making progress with that pattern, go in the other direction. So few of us change direction when we see the tree the second time.

We don't recognize or acknowledge we are walking in a circle, and if we don't change direction we aren't going to get where we're going. The first indication is our best opportunity to make a change, to go a different way. Once we've seen the tree the third time, it's very likely a

> When you are wandering through the proverbial forest and you see a tree you recognize, make note of it. If you see that tree again, it's because you're walking in a circle.

habit or pattern has formed, and we will continue to walk in a circle. We're going to continue to do the thing we've always done.

Ditching the Security Blanket

Once I had learned about the tree experience and realized how to identify my habits and patterns and decided to go a different direction, it changed my life immeasurably. This lesson is especially helpful to me because I enjoy comfort and familiarity.

In many ways I rely upon it. Like so many of us, I am a creature of habit and wear my rituals like a security blanket. One example was in my personal relationships. I am someone who struggles with trust and abandonment issues. It's a real challenge I am working through as I get older. I am prone to hold on to people and things that no longer serve me.

When I was younger, I would find myself returning to old relationships because they were familiar and safe, even if I knew they wouldn't last and weren't the best for me. I struggled to leave harmful relationships because the alternative, the unknown, was so much scarier. We often rely on habits and patterns for protection, not realizing our security blanket, that comfort, may be trapping us and holding us down.

> But if you've ever said, "every time I [do this], then [this happens]," then you have had a tree experience.

Tree experiences, the realization you have encountered a situation before, are important signposts, an invitation and opportunity to do something different. A tree can show up in many different ways in your life, but if you've ever said, "every time I [do this], then [this happens]," then you have had a tree experience.

One example is staying in a job that doesn't bring you joy or use your skills fully because it pays well. This is likely a tree of fear and insecurity, which shows up whenever you feel ready to switch careers or apply for a promotion. If, whenever you plan a vacation or self-care time, you don't schedule it because you don't have time or don't want to spend the money, this could be a tree of guilt or low self-worth.

My advice: take that vacation, leave that relationship, and apply for that position. The tree you keep seeing is signaling to you that you need to go in a different direction. That one change could make a significant decision, setting you on different path and a different outcome.

CHANGE "ONE" THING

The final step in the ABCs to living life on purpose is "C" for change. Though change is a necessary part of life, change can be a scary concept. Just hearing the word "change" can make your heartbeat faster and your palms sweat. The pandemic forced most of us to make significant changes, and many of those experiences were negative and overwhelming. But not all change is bad.

> Author Octavia Butler said, "Everything you touch, you change. Everything you change changes you."

Change can be a positive thing, particularly when we use it to our advantage. I teach leaders to embrace change and unlock their power to change the world in small and large ways. Challenge your belief that change is a massive, 360-degree transformation that turns the entire world upside down.

Change doesn't have to be a big, destabilizing undertaking. Change doesn't have to be monumental. Change one thing. Author Octavia Butler said, "Everything you touch, you change. Everything you change changes you." Start by making the commitment to change one thing.

That one thing creates a ripple in the pond that becomes a wave. Start with one small pebble. Decide you are going to take a different route to work. You will see something you've never seen before. It will change your perspective.

If you typically sleep in, wake up an hour earlier. If you go to bed late, go to bed an hour earlier. You may see the sun rise for the first time or get the extra rest your need to face the challenges of the day.

Take a day off and use the time for reflection and self-care. Apply for the position you've been dreaming about, even if you don't meet all the listed requirements. Take the hobby you've wanted to turn into a business and start working on your business plan. Take that spinning class you've wanted to take. Join that weekly wine group you've been thinking about for years. Making that one change can get you closer to your purpose.

Change as Good

Let's commit to seeing change as positive, not automatically negative. It's all about perspective. Mindset matters. Whenever I feel overwhelmed or upset because I must do something, I think about all the people who would love to be doing what I am doing. I also recall the times when I prayed or wished for the very thing I don't want to do, and it makes me grateful for the things I once complained about.

On the advice of a good friend, I changed my "gots" to "gets." Instead of saying, "I've got to go to work today," I say, "I get to go to work today." Guess what? Nothing about my day has changed. I still have to go to work, but that mindset shift to one of gratitude changes my perspective. In the same way, change your outlook on change. Approach change like you would any other habit you are trying to shift, with practice and patience. Over time, change won't seem so frightening because you will get used to it. You adjust. You might actually like it.

> On the advice of a good friend, I changed my "gots" to "gets."

I have reinvented myself at least six times in my twenty-year career. The first time I made a shift was difficult, and the learning curve was steep. Going from full-time legal practice to working as a college administrator and professor was an adjustment. Everything was different. My work schedule, pay and benefits, reporting structure, work environment—it all changed.

As a self-diagnosed control freak, I approached that change very cautiously. I had to work through my budget carefully, since I was making 50% less pay. I had to adjust my sleep and travel schedule for the longer commute and earlier start.

Not all the adjustments were negative. I got to advance my retirement goals because public employees have generous retirement benefits. I had free weekends and a month in the summer to devote to other hobbies and interests. I was given so much more flexibility—no more billing hours and face time in the office on weekends. I gained freedom because my boss really trusted me to build the program and gave me latitude, leeway, and lots of support.

Before transitioning to higher education, I would not have valued freedom or time over salary. That experience changed my perspective, opening the door to my next couple of moves. Once I realized I could live on less, and that my time and freedom were priceless, I was more than comfortable taking a public service job five years later, which was a lateral move financially but certainly a role consistent with my purpose.

The best part is I am now in a place where I am making more money and also have a job that gives me freedom and allows me to control my time and work schedule so I can have a fuller, richer life. And it all started with that very first change.

Take a moment now and think about a few things in your life that if you changed them would change the way you navigate the world in a way that positively impacts you. The thing you wish to change doesn't have to be something big, but the changing of the thing has an impact that is important. Maybe you want to wake up earlier. Maybe you could benefit from staying up later at night. Perhaps you have wanted to reserve an hour each day to write or spend one less hour each day doom-scrolling on social media. Write those things down now.

Make a list of no more than ten things to start. Once you've completed that initial list, choose one thing, just one, you are going to change this week. Remember you are not trying to tackle the entire list, but instead you are going to change just one thing. That may not feel monumental, but the interesting thing about change is once you realize you can change one thing you realize you can change so much more.

"CHANGE ONE THING" EXERCISE

LIVING "ON PURPOSE"

There is another meaning behind "Living Life on Purpose." It's the idea that we have the power to decide what we do and control how we live. We've revisited this idea of agency a couple of times in this book—when we realize the power, we have to make choices, and it's pretty amazing, really! In addition to living in power, you must also harness the idea of intention. You can indeed live "on purpose," that is to say, with intention.

So much of that is about how we allow the world and the circumstances and people around us to tell us what we can and cannot do, what we should and shouldn't do. Like living a purpose-driven life, this is not something we are born with; this is something we are conditioned to do.

Take for example a newborn. If an infant wants something, that intention is everything to them. If they want to sleep, they sleep. When they are ready to eat, they let you know they want to eat. Time to go to the bathroom? You get the idea.

As children grow and become toddlers, they enter the stage we refer to as the "terrible twos." Parents teach them boundaries and limitations. Kids will say, "I want to go to the playground now." We tell them, "Not right now, honey. Let's learn our ABCs first, and then we will have time for play."

From those interactions, kids learn there is a time and a way we do things. For different families and cultures those things look different. Think about how kids who live in urban environments have a different set of norms and rituals, standards, and rules than kids in rural areas.

If you were raised to wake up before dawn to feed the cattle, your life, your view of what you should do and must do, the habits and standards you develop will look different than a kid who wakes up a little later and the first thing they do is have breakfast and get dressed for school. In a global context, think about how culturally different our sense of ritual and standard, habit, custom, boundaries, and limitations can impact the way we view what's possible.

Being raised by my grandmother, we had plenty of boundaries. My grandmother had her rules, and you followed them, in part because the consequences were swift and painful but also because we were raised that you respected your elders, your parents, and what they said, you did, no questions and no backtalk.

So, I grew up, pretty much, as a rule follower. I didn't love suffering consequences and wanted my grandmother to be proud of me. I never wanted to be a bother, so I tried my best to be a "good girl." Mostly. As I mentioned before, I was what my grandmother called an "old soul." She said she looked into my eyes when I was born and knew I had lived on this earth before.

Even then I had an independent streak. I was left-handed, and in my generation right-handed scissors were the norm. I wasn't comfortable using them and didn't want to force myself to do something I wasn't comfortable doing just because someone said I should. So, I refused. Eventually, after I resisted and persisted, my teacher relented. I was allowed to use left-handed scissors.

Over time, I began to embrace my left-handedness and decided to lean into my distinctive trait and see it as a value rather than a deficit. To this day I've learned to do things left-handed. Seems like a simple thing, but learning to play golf, tennis, baseball, and guitar left-handed was measurably more difficult, sometimes requiring different equipment and learning to shadow my instructors, all of whom were right-handed.

> Somewhere in our development, we lose our sense of independence, our sense of adventure, our sense of self.

This was just one early example of how I decided I was going to live my life on my own terms. Unfortunately, as we get older, the stakes are higher. For those who aren't naturally inclined to buck the system, resist, or stand up and stand out, this can be even more difficult.

The world requires us to follow the rules and give into systematic ways of living. Working nine to five, which was much more customary decades ago, required people with different circadian rhythms to adapt to a strict morning schedule, and people with different learning and implementation abilities needed to adapt to traditional expectations of timeliness.

It's no wonder people, after spending years of working in jobs they don't love and that don't bring them joy, are deciding to "reinvent themselves," "retire and rewire," and begin a "second act."

From my years as a preprofessional adviser to my work now as an executive strategist, adviser, and coach, I encounter people trying to "figure out" who they are and who they are meant to be. Somewhere in our development, we lose our sense of independence, our sense of adventure, our sense of self. We are told our dreams aren't practical, the things we want to do can't be done, or we must make sacrifices to achieve the things we want to do.

Imagine a little girl who wants to be a dancer when she is young. She takes lessons, practices, and competes. She is very good, and as she grows older she continues to lean into dance, her gift, and her passion. She trains under some of the best dancers in middle and high school, dedicating every free moment to practice and perfecting her craft.

Her parents and instructors continue to encourage her and help her become a beautiful, talented dancer, capable of performing on the biggest and best stages. They invest time and money, supporting her every step of the way. As she prepares to enter college, she begins researching schools with top-notch dance programs. At this point, her counselor at school and her parents decide to give her some practical advice. As talented as she is, the prospect of "making it" as a professional dancer are very slim.

They encourage her to consider a more a "practical" career path, one that is more secure and likely. Perhaps one where she can "make a good living." She can continue to dance for fun, as a hobby. So, based on their advice, rather than continuing down the path of her dream, she decides to "play it safe" and select a major and a school that allows her to graduate with more security, or at least that's what she tells herself. She can continue her dancing while in school, and if she is meant to do it, it will work out.

Once she enrolls in college, the demands of her studies make time for dancing less available. Eventually, after a few months of failing at the balancing act, she gives up on her dream of dancing, opting instead for a prosperous and respectable career in dentistry. After twenty years, she rarely thinks about the world she left behind, except when she goes to the ballet or a movie or show with a featured dancer. Then she wonders whether she could have made it as a dancer and regrets her decision to play it safe.

This story is so common. Young adults are conditioned to push down their dreams and gifts to do something very practical instead. That reaches far past the decision of what they want to be when we grow up and into decisions about when and whether we to get married, have a family, spend free time, and which leadership opportunities to pursue.

Even more impactful and far more subtly, being conditioned to the practical, over time and after years of making the safe choice, makes people believe they have no control over their present or their future decisions. Those decisions become habits, and habits become lifestyle. Diverting from them, even in the slightest way, feels far too onerous and ultimately not worth the risk or the effort. That leads people to believe that life happens "to them," and they don't have control over their lives and decisions.

Over time, small choices, like driving a different way to work, or getting up thirty minutes later, or trying a new recipe or dance class feels out of reach. It keeps people trapped, and in many cases, keeps them from living a life they deserve. What's worse, it robs the world of people living their lives fully, passionately, and on purpose.

When I speak with executives considering taking a more elevated role, their first concern is almost always how the new role will change their present circumstances. Not the excitement of taking on a new challenge, the validation of their excellent performance with even more responsibility and more resources. The idea of changing their work routine, adjusting their life circumstances, and more pointedly, the fear of all the things that would change often stirs up feelings of insecurity and anxiety in a situation that should, at least initially, spark feelings of accomplishment and excitement.

> Imagine if every time you are faced with an opportunity you see the possibilities before you consider the challenges.

In my work, I remind leaders they have control over every decision they make and how they react to what happens in their lives. That power is something we all possess, one that cannot be taken away. As we get older and our lives get more complicated, in some cases more comfortable, we inhibit our own power by allowing the fear of change or the prospect of losing what we have to keep us from exercising that power.

To be clear, for some of us, this isn't a power we are happy to acknowledge or exercise. Every decision we make has an outcome, which could be positive or negative. Often, we convince ourselves something bad will happen, and we opt to not make the decision. That makes us feel powerless, and we tell ourselves we don't have a choice or can't do something when we have simply talked ourselves out of making a choice. I work to empower people to make decisions, own them, and see them as opportunities rather than obstacles.

Imagine if every time you are faced with an opportunity you see the possibilities before you consider the challenges. What if you didn't allow fear or excuses to keep you from moving forward? What if you acknowledged and then calculated risk or weighed it accurately rather than seeing any risk as a disqualification, a "no go," or a reason not to proceed at all?

THE KEYS TO LIVING ON PURPOSE

Intention

There are several keys to living "on purpose." The first is intention. The word "intent" means "to be resolved or determined to do something." Intention is defined as "anything intended or planned; aim, end, purpose."

> The word "intent" means "to be resolved or determined to do something." Intention is defined as "anything intended or planned; aim, end, purpose."

We must first decide we want to do something before we can actually do it. Simple and easy, right? Well, this first step is often the hardest. We live our lives like machines in a constant state of "go, go, go," and we see our habits as essential to getting through the day, the week, the month, and the year.

To be clear, some rituals and habits are helpful. For instance, it serves everyone when I brush my teeth and shower daily. You should feed yourself when you are hungry, and going to bed and getting sleep every day is a must. But never forget even these habits are decisions you make and can change. You can, and some people do, decide not to do these "daily practices" every day.

There are times when we prioritize some things over those things we've trained ourselves to do every day. That prioritization is intention. Many of us take the same route to work every day. You can decide to take a different way to work. You can wake up and decide you are not going to work at all.

When you realize you have the power to make the choices you make in your life, you can also make the very important decision to do something different or nothing at all. When doing this, it is best to start with the small stuff, because it can be overwhelming to think about switching careers if you haven't yet wrapped your head around taking just one day off from work. It's one of the reasons why, as we discussed earlier, we start with changing just one thing rather than changing everything at once.

You Choose

Put more simply, intention is just a fancy word for making up your mind to do something or not do something. You decide. You make a choice.

So, what is the thing you want to do or have that you aren't doing or don't have right now? In other words, what is your goal? Setting a real, concrete goal is the first step to living life "on purpose." The word "goal" can feel overwhelming and intimidating.

> Intention is just a fancy word for making up your mind to do something or not do something. You decide. You make a choice.

We think goals must be big things. Sometimes they are. When we set career goals or life-planning goals, they are big, long-term goals that will take many steps and often a long time to accomplish. But they don't have to be. You can intend or have a goal to make dinner this evening. Yes, you can set a goal to get food, preferably edible and delicious, to put on the dinner table on time.

Depending on how your life schedule works currently, and the systems and tools you have at your disposal, that may be an easy feat or a difficult one. Setting that goal will require you to adjust your routine and do things differently. You will have to make time to get groceries. You must make sure you have the tools to make the meal you want: food processor, pots and pans, utensils. You must set aside time to prep your ingredients. And you must allocate time to cook and serve the meal.

Those things can only happen once you set your intention, make your goal, and adjust your schedule and routine to accommodate this objective. The larger your goal, the more things you must plan for and adjust.

Say, for instance, you want to be promoted at work within the next year. The next level job requires different skills than the job you currently have. You will need to make a plan to prepare yourself for the new role while you continue to excel in your current one. Your goal may, for instance, require additional training, which means you may need to adjust your schedule, which may require you to stop doing something else or extend your day and get less sleep. It may require you to get more help around the house or with childcare if you have a family.

All those changes start with you deciding, setting your intention to get a promotion.

Intention requires imagination and vision, especially if your plate is already full. It requires faith, hopefulness, and optimism. You must see yourself differently, bigger, and better. It also takes energy, dedication, and relentlessness.

Remember how when I was eight years old I decided I wanted to be a lawyer? I had to have vision to see that far ahead and faith to dream that big. Once I got to college, I had to put in the work to achieve academically so I could get admitted to law school. In law school, I spent most of my time sacrificing my personal life and sleep to study.

I had to spend resources for the degree, books, study materials. But when I went back to school to get my MBA ten years later, it was even more difficult. Why? Because I was working two jobs, I had a mortgage and a car-loan payment. I had even less time for classes and studying. So I joined an executive program designed for busy professionals.

> You must fix your heart on the goal and your mind on the how, and your hands and feet must be committed to "do."

Intention requires both vision and practice, that we dream and believe ahead while we do the work. Intention is about so much more than a dream, but it requires a long-term perspective because you are almost certainly setting your intention on something that doesn't currently exist. You must fix your heart on the goal and your mind on the how, and your hands and feet must be committed to "do."

So many people get stuck and never advance because they get so consumed with the right now, they can't imagine how they will ever be able to get to the next thing. Others are able to dream but get stuck, overwhelmed by all the twists and turns, ups and downs, hurdles and roadblocks it takes to get from here to there.

Execution

Once you have set your intention, large or small, next you have to focus on execution. This is where my practical and logical folks shine. Mostly. There are people who are hardwired to "do, do, do." We call them task masters, people who can follow a prompt and execute it perfectly. Once they have a direction, they're like a dog with a bone—working the goal. There is only one problem with that.

In any journey, as you are plugging away, checking the boxes, doing the things, there will certainly be a variable, something you didn't expect, a twist. Pay attention. You may need to stop executing, evaluate the new situation and circumstances, find a new direction, then get back at it.

For those who are naturally good at executing on a plan, unexpected shifts can create anxiety, fear, and confusion. When I work with strong, detail-oriented leaders, I start by working with them on scenario planning.

Choose Your Own Adventure

Mapping out and working through all the possible outcomes so they can see all the things that could stand in the way of getting from A to B is the sweet spot for "doers." What happens if you submit the proposal and the very foundation of your work, the reason or premise the work is founded upon, is challenged or rejected? What will you do then? Can you adjust from there? Do you go back to square one? How do you plan ahead in case that happens.

I remember as a kid loving games like Oregon Trail and Choose Your Own Adventure. I guess I've always been a hybrid person—vision + execution—which makes me a pretty good problem solver. But most people are better at one or the other. When that is the case, you have to spend the time and make the commitment to practice and prepare for whichever one is your natural weakness.

When I was working as an aide in the Judicial Affairs office of my law school alma mater, one of my jobs was conducting training for our "repeat offenders," students who had made several poor choices, leading them to multiple, recurring violations of the Student Code of Conduct. I was tasked with helping them understand how their decisions and choices were leading them down the wrong path, and I taught them how to think ahead, to really ask themselves how they would react when faced with a certain scenario, one where they could avoid a similar negative outcome.

For instance, I would have students imagine they were at a party with friends, and they were all drinking. In this scenario, the person driving was really drunk, and they all were too impaired to drive. "What would you do in this situation?" I'd ask.

Inevitably, students most commonly responded that whichever of their friends was the least intoxicated should drive the others home. Side note— No. Absolutely not! But this is their lesson, so I let them choose their own adventure. "Ok. Let's say that happens, and on the way home a pedestrian runs in front of the car and the driver hits the pedestrian.

What would you do then? Assume that no one is around and the police haven't been called. What are you going to do as a passenger in the car, knowing that every one of you has had too much to drink? What if the person is severely injured or dead? What do you do? Do you call 911 and render aid? Do you run away?

Are you the one who steps up and influences the others to "do the right thing" as they contemplate leaving or pointing the finger at one another?" After we worked through at least five scenarios, the situation getting worse and more difficult, we'd take a step back. First, what is motivating your decision-making here? What values are you relying on in your decision-making?

Through this process, I helped them think through and develop their personal code and identify rules they will live by, those foundational principles that will prove essential when difficult, especially life-altering decisions have to be made in an instant. Have you ever done an exercise like this? Have you thought about how you would respond in a stressful, dangerous, or fatal situation?

Are you someone who speaks up, even when it's not a popular position? Are you someone who tells the truth, even if it could hurt you and your future? Are you a "good Samaritan," someone who will care for a person in need even if it's inconvenient or costs you everything?

Perhaps you should consider developing a personal code for your own life. By helping my students establish a personal code, I helped them prepare for the things in life that might throw them off track and, in some cases, derail their future success.

From A to Backup Plan

People who are A-to-B people, executors, or doers, will benefit from thinking about how things might go wrong or even right on their journey. During my run for mayor, I wouldn't allow myself to think about what I would do if I didn't win. Against my natural and better judgment, I didn't create a Plan B. I wouldn't allow myself to because I feared it would allow me to give less than 100% to the race, to have an escape plan that would allow me to quit when things got tough—which they did, so many times.

As someone who is a visionary who is also good at execution, creating back-up plans is second nature to me, so sometimes I get distracted by the alternatives when my primary assignment hits a stumbling block or a delay. But this time, I didn't create a back-up plan. After that loss, I was not prepared for how long and tough transitioning to something new would be.

My lack of planning caused the devastation to turn quickly to fear and anxiety. It took me seven months to re-envision what was possible for my future outside of political leadership. I'd always prepared for what I'd do next, so this was a first for me.

I remember graduating from law school and thinking, alright … I'm going to work at a law firm, make partner, and maybe become a judge someday. Not that novel, considering this is a very traditional path for lawyers, but I had a plan in place from the moment I entered the profession. The alternative was to work for a few years in private practice, go in-house with a company, retire, then run a non-profit as my giveback during my twilight years.

It was difficult during that time when people asked me what I was going to do next and I didn't have an answer. It really took me out of my comfort zone and created an urgency and anxiety I wasn't prepared for.

Fortunately, by this point in my career, I was already pretty good at reinventing myself.

For someone who doesn't think or plan their career in advance but instead focuses on the task at hand, the role they are in at the present moment or the prospect of losing their job could be just enough to paralyze them, to make them want to quit or give up. So I reinforce with leaders the importance of getting tasks done and doing them well, while also coaching and preparing them to pivot and adjust when the world around them shifts, because it certainly will. The only constant, the only thing we can be sure of, is that things will change. I find it best to know and accept that and be ready when it does.

> If you stay ready, you don't have to get ready.

Execution requires looking ahead, because if you don't you will remain in the same place or, worse, get behind. If a leader wants to be promoted, they must execute on their current tasks and responsibilities while training for the next position. "If you stay ready, you don't have to get ready."

Excellence

Living in your purpose requires a commitment to excellence. That commitment will yield so much positive fruit. Some of that fruit will be evident to you in the form of more power, money, responsibility, time, freedom—all sorts of things.

What's more, your excellence will positively impact others in ways you might never know about. I hope, however, that you'll get glimpses of it from time to time. I remember one of my first days as a council member. I was sitting on the dais and after the meeting, as I walked down to head back to my office, a young girl approached me with her mother. She was around thirteen years old; I could tell because she had that look—a cute little bow popping in her hair, a little bling on her wrist, color popping in the shoe. Total pre-teen energy.

She walked up and said, "You are beautiful, and you inspire me." Wow! I was immediately overcome with emotion; I could barely speak. At that moment, I realized that being in that role was about so much more than just doing a job. There were little girls (and boys) watching me, and I was an inspiration to them. I had to model excellence for them. As a leader, your work is always bigger than you.

Excellence isn't perfection, but it's better than good. Excellence isn't about being great; it's about being your very best. Few people really understand what it takes to excel. When I work with leaders, I distinguish between what it means to have natural talent, intellect, and skill and the work it takes to excel.

Excellence requires intention and execution, but it also requires the commitment to be extraordinary. Becoming excellent is within your power; it's something you can work to attain. When I think about excellence, I think about Jesse Owens, one the fastest men of all time, a track and field champion and an Olympian.

Jesse was fast, and there was very little question about his talent and ability on the track. But becoming a champion takes more than natural ability, talent, or skill. It takes hard work, consistent practice, and a commitment to get better, even when you are already great at something. The difference between good leaders and great ones is hard work, discipline, and practice.

If you are doing purpose-driven work, which is important work, it demands your commitment to excellence. Doing work that brings you joy, that is consistent with your purpose, and uses your most authentic gifts and talents also requires your best. So many people believe that if you are operating in your purpose, you are all good.

> Doing work that brings you joy, that is consistent with your purpose, and uses your most authentic gifts and talents also requires your best.

But the Jesse Owens example illustrates that being good at something and doing it isn't enough. Excellence requires hard work, sharpening those innate skills, the things we are naturally good at. Basketball coach John Wooden said, "Champions are brilliant at the basics."

You not only have to be excellent at your core function—sales, medicine, law—you must also have a broad range of skills outside your main job.

When I worked as a local political leader, I already had a law degree and had proven myself as a leader in the profession, but I noticed there were parts of my job that I wasn't proficient in. As a litigator and legal counsel, I had to become an expert at whatever the subject matter was so I could understand my client's business to advise them and, if litigation ensued, make the case for them. So, I became adept at learning new things quickly.

Once I became Vice Chair of the Budget and Finance Committee at Cincinnati City Hall, I realized there was a lot about the process of managing a $1.2 billion city budget that required experience I didn't have. Understanding bonds and other financial instruments, the accounting process, and concepts like structural balance, and in economics how the government impacts and is impacted by larger economic factors would help me execute my role even more effectively. So I went back to school to get my MBA.

> Our work is a continuum and as things change around us, we have an opportunity to grow and change with it.

Because public service was my calling, my purpose, and my job impacted so many people, including the 300,000 people who lived in my city and the 2.1 million people who used our city services every day, it was important to me that I learn everything I could to be excellent at my job.

The truth is that no matter what profession you are in, the people you serve deserve your very best, so training and educating yourself so that you are the very best is essential to being a leader of excellence. Many leaders get complacent in their work. They have been doing it for a while and think they know everything they need to do and how to do it. They come in every day, they do their job, and they go home.

But they don't appreciate how important it is to "sharpen your saw" regularly. When I advise and train leaders, I reinforce the premise that our work is a continuum and as things change around us, we have an opportunity to grow and change with it. When social media became a new, essential part of our lives, there was a lot of resistance among leaders to this new technology.

So many executives rejected learning social media, instead hiring young people to manage their social media for them. To be clear, there is nothing wrong with hiring people who are skilled at an area that isn't your core strength. But refusing to learn a skill that is essential to your purpose is counterproductive to excellence.

Intuition

"Don't overthink it. What is your gut telling you?" Living "on purpose" requires listening to and trusting the little voice in your spirit, that natural inclination, the thing that tells you to stop, or go, or tells you to wait. We call that intuition. Intuition is defined as: "the ability to understand something immediately without the need for conscious reasoning."

You have it, you hear it, but do you listen? Intuition is intrinsic and personal and a safety valve for each of us as we navigate our lives. It's a major part of intention because it acts as a barometer, a compass, or even a traffic signal. It gives us insights as we are on our journey that tell us when and where to go, and oftentimes when and where not to go.

> Intuition is defined as: "the ability to understand something immediately without the need for conscious reasoning."

When we are younger, we lean more on instincts than our intellect. We are closer to what we feel, our inner nature, because we haven't had experiences that cause us to distrust ourselves. Experiences, especially difficult and challenging circumstances and events can lead to self-doubt, which is the root of distrust.

Before we know it, we have replaced our natural innate instincts with analysis, which is often resistant, reserved, and dismissive. Have you ever encountered a person who can't make a decision? They are haunted by analysis paralysis, afraid to make a bad decision. They shut down their instincts and stop trusting their gut. So they either overanalyze every single decision, and when that doesn't work they act out of pure reactive emotion.

To be clear, intellect can serve as a guard and protector, the rational brain helping you dissect very complicated decisions. It can also block you from doing things you are meant to do, keep you from taking important risks, and trusting the part of yourself that allows and encourages us to chart new paths that are important to fulfilling your purpose.

We are complete beings, made up of our heads (intellect), our hearts (feelings and emotions), and our guts (our intuition). I recall a conversation I had years ago with a good friend when I was contemplating ending a romantic relationship. He gave me the best advice and said, "Yvette, you know what your problem is? You let your head do heart things, and your heart do head things."

"Yvette, you know what your problem is? You let your head do heart things, and your heart do head things."

He was telling me I was allowing my emotions to guide my career path, and I was overthinking my relationship, allowing my brain to guide something my heart should be directing. In the midst of all of that, I was totally ignoring my instincts, which often serves as the referee when there is a conflict between my head and my heart.

Trust Your Gut

When we don't trust our instincts, it can cause us to freeze or retreat. A big part of intention requires us to own our power to make decisions, to take a step forward even when we can't see the ground ahead of us, even when we don't know what's next.

Instincts are instrumental to intention because it fills the gap between what we see and what we can't yet see. It allows us to draw on what we know about ourselves and what we believe is possible for us. Our intuition is personal. It belongs just to us, and because of this we should trust it.

But many of us treat our instincts as a stranger, this nagging voice that is trying to make us do something we shouldn't or can't. We treat it as an external adviser rather than an internal inkling. Your intuition sounds like you because it is you. And because it exists on the other side of our consciousness, it is the purest version of you. It persists without filter but is inclusive of our experiences and memories, good and bad.

Listen to that pull, that tug, that feeling inside you telling you to move. Yes, you can and should take in all the available information before making a decision. You should certainly check in with your emotions if the decision is a personal one, and your head if it is a professional one. But at the end of the day, if your gut is rumbling, listen to it. Let your intuition fill the gap between your head and your heart.

> Listen to that pull, that tug, that feeling inside you telling you to move.

Your gut can also be your grounding force. It can also give you wings. But it should be treated as a valid, important, and integral part of your decision-making system. Don't subordinate your instinct. Trust your gut, and let it lead you down the path to changing the things you need to change to fulfill your purpose.

You've now got the keys to unlock the door to your future. With intention, execution, excellence, and intuition, you can fulfill your purpose.

CLOSING THOUGHTS: LET THE JOURNEY BEGIN

Years ago, I was visiting a great friend, who has since passed away, in Nashville, Tennessee. After she showed me around her new home, we ventured out and into a cute little bookstore with a coffee shop.

I am always on the hunt for a new and fresh journal in which to place my thoughts and ideas. I feel that when I am on the hunt for journals or books or any kind of inspiration, the one meant for me will find me. This day was no exception. I walked over to the section of the store where they kept journals. There I found a white journal with black writing.

> Purpose, like happiness, is a pursuit that occurs over a lifetime.

The front of the journal read, "Happiness is a journey, not a destination." What a revelation! It was just the message I needed in that moment. The idea that happiness is not a place, a time, or even a thing but instead a journey—full of hills and valleys, fits and starts, and a thing to pursue, not to be pursued—was just the message I needed at the time.

The same is true for purpose. Many believe that living your purpose is something you can achieve—as if, once you're there, you're there. That hasn't been my experience. Purpose, like happiness, is a pursuit that occurs over a lifetime.

The pursuit of purpose can be redeeming and uplifting, but it can also be confounding and humbling. Just when you think you've figured it out, you realize that you have reached yet another turn in the journey. The pursuit of purpose, like happiness, is what life is about. Along the journey, we discover more about ourselves and the world around us. We discover we will need new wisdom, new lessons, and new tools for the next stage of the journey.

One thing I know for certain is the world has everything it needs, especially when we are all operating in our purpose and doing that authentically. If you get to the place you're destined to be, it's because someone is waiting there for you who needs exactly you in that moment. I call that "standing on the X."

As I write these words, I am in the midst of another shift, another turn in the journey, one I didn't expect when I began writing this book. Another door has closed, and I am in the process of looking for the open window on the other side of the room once again. I know this shift is destined and will lead me closer to fulfillment, to work that brings me joy, and a new way to use my gifts, talents, and my passion for good.

> One thing I know for certain is the world has everything it needs, especially when we are all operating in our purpose and doing that authentically.

Legacy, after all, is a long game, a roller coaster with lots of ups and downs, twists and turns. You can approach that ride with fear, grasping to the lap bar tightly and screaming in terror the whole way, sure, but it's so much more fun to let go, lift your hands, laugh, and enjoy the ride.

So I approach the ride with openness, looking for opportunity, rather than with fear and consternation. I anticipate the next leg of this reinvention journey with anticipation, possibility, and optimism. I'm excited to see where it leads me this time.

I believe fundamentally the world needs people operating *on purpose.*

The key to living "on purpose" is understanding that as you get closer to the work that makes you come alive, the work that is your North Star, that brings you joy, as you get closer to standing on the "X" and being in the place where people who need you are waiting for you, you will find fulfillment for you and others connected to their purpose.

The world needs more people who "come alive" because our worlds, our destinies, our missions are intertwined. Too many in our culture and our world are obsessed with the extremes of insufficiency and abundance—assuming that life is about having more.

Such a belief leads to the pursuit of "more" rather than the pursuit of what will fulfill and sustain you. I firmly believe that we have everything we need *in one another*. When we each operate as optimally as we can, in positions that are our "purpose" in a way that is "on purpose," we have balance—we will have everything we need.

> When you can see your world a different way, you'll soon realize you have the power to change your life and even the world.

Open your mind to something more. It might feel like a big leap, but it can be as simple as just a step. Entering into a life on purpose requires you change just one thing, step outside of your routine and your comfort zone, and do something different. Taking that single step will change everything—starting with your perspective. When you can see your world a different way, you'll soon realize you have the power to change your life and even the world.

That's living in intention. Take that first step, setting your mind and heart on doing that very thing. Opportunities that you never imagined will enter into your orbit. You'll see the world differently, and the world will see you differently. As you live on purpose authentically and with intention, you'll radiate in ways that are attractive and magnetic. That energy will open doors and windows that were previously closed.

And that, my friends, is what living on purpose looks like. It's a beautiful thing.

IN GRATITUDE

Few of us get very far down the path of life without a village of people to support them. In my introductory "I Am" poem, I write about being born in a village on a street named "Love," and the truth is, I am one of those fortunate people who has had people help me navigate and survive the treacherous path of life from pillar to post and back again.

I realize it's a dangerous exercise to begin the process of specifically naming people, so I will start by acknowledging that this is not a complete list of everyone who has been a village and support to me, and know that if you are not referenced here, I still have your name on my heart.

God.

I have to start by thanking God. I was raised in the Baptist church, Friendship Baptist Church, in my hometown of Lincoln Heights, Ohio, which, outside my home, was my first village. I was raised with faith and a belief that the world we live in isn't ours alone but is a gift from God.

I was raised that all blessings come from God and that we should give him all the glory, honor, and praise. I know I was blessed with so many gifts, including the gift of wisdom and insight, which has directed my life's path since I was a child, but also with resilience, strength, and compassion, all foundational parts of my being. I thank God for all of that and more. In my weakest and darkest moments, which I assure you are many, it is my faith in God that sustains me and allows me to push through. Thank you, Lord.

Family.

I thanked my grandmother and my sister in the introduction, but I want to acknowledge my entire family, who have all played a part in molding the person I have become. The Simpson family is a strong, determined, and loving group of people. We are not perfect. But we persevere. Sometimes we have to cry, laugh, and line dance our way through it, but we get there.

Like most families, we love hard, and we fight harder, only to love each other again. In my life, I have always been able to lean on my family to get me through. I won't name any specific names, but if you ever fed or clothed me, looked after me, housed me, encouraged me or supported me, bragged about me, danced or sang karaoke with me, family—I love you.

I am proud to be a Simpson girl, and I realize the responsibility that comes with carrying that name. The Bailey family, my father's clan, has been a rock for me throughout my life. Like the Simpsons, the women in the family are strong and caring and would give you everything they have.

When I wasn't sleeping on a couch or a spare bedroom with the Simpsons, I was certainly at a Bailey house. Never asked for a thing, always giving, I see my reflection in my cousins and aunts, and I appreciate the way they nurtured me and kept me, even when my father wasn't able to.

My grandfather brought me in, and they received me. We have fun and laugh and joke in our own way, and when the going gets tough or there is any reason to celebrate, we come together. Thank you, Bailey family, for welcoming me as your own.

I was fortunate to find a true love in this life, and it has made me a better person, a better giver, and a more authentic and anchored soul. As much as I am a Simpson and a Bailey, I am a Hoffecker.

My husband and I met and married later in life, and his family quickly became my own. For so many reasons, that was supposed to be more difficult than it turned out to be—but it wasn't. I was immediately embraced by the Hoffecker-Fisher clan and loved like I was one of the family, and I have grown and learned so much from each one of them.

The Hoffeckers are a lot like the Simpsons and the Baileys, a strong family who loves to be together through the good and bad times. We stick together and support each other no matter what, and the love, the food, and the libations flow continually.

With my marriage, I inherited three bonus daughters, a sister, and two brothers, six nieces and seven nephews, and several great nieces, along with a host of cousins and "framily" (friends who are like family) who came along with the package. Thank you, all of you.

Framily.

Speaking of framily, they say you have the family that you're born with and the family you choose. I have been so fortunate to have, since I was young, so many people in my life who have been there for me through thick and thin.

From my best friends in elementary school who were there when I decided what I wanted to be when I grew up, another who I watched *Teen Jeopardy* with and bought and raised "Sea Monkeys" with, to my Double Dutch coach, family, and teammates who taught me the importance of teamwork and hard work, and how to win and lose.

My teachers, who saw something in me that I didn't see in myself, and mentors and principals, who understood what I was up against, stepped in and pulled me out, allowing me to reach for the stars and accomplish my greatest dreams and achievements. Teachers are everything, and we must respect, appreciate, and pay teachers what they are worth. This is my one soapbox moment, and I won't apologize. Thank you.

Mentors and Mamas.

In my Ted Talk, I talk about the "mentors and mamas" who made me who I am. There are a whole host of them, from childhood to today, who have invested time, resources, wisdom, and advice whenever I call, who remind me who I am and what I have overcome, just to show me what I am capable of doing in the future. I am so grateful to each of you.

Some come in the form of true mentors—my personal "Board of Advisors." Others are like sister- or brother-friends—we navigate life together with the boomerang of advice that we pass back and forth so often we can't recall where it originated.

Others are spiritual guides and advisors who keep my spirit lifted and my soul anchored. In many ways, you are the stitching in the quilt and the mortar between the bricks. You keep me together. Thank you.

The Sisterhood.

And then there is my college crew. The sisters I met in college are my support and backbone now. A crew of fun, smart, loving women who were my perfect match. We dreamed about our futures and encouraged each other to accomplish our goals.

The sleepovers and the singing and dancing—I mean, it was the 90s, and music was everything then. I remember them kidnapping me once because I was doing too much—some things never change—so that I could have some time away from my many majors and activities.

This was before self-care was a thing, but my sisters knew I needed it, and I'm so grateful they did. We all pledged our beloved sorority, Delta Sigma Theta Sorority, Inc.—though at different times and different places—and we have supported one another through moves across the country, weddings, children, graduations—so many graduations, new jobs, and promotions—the good and bad of life. Thank you.

The Friend Circle.

As a young professional, I thought for sure my "friend door" was closed. I just assumed we reached an age where we were too old to make new friends. I am so glad I was wrong about that. I have, since college, accumulated an amazing band of sisters and brothers as a whole adult that have sustained me to now through all of life's swift transitions.

A mentee who has become a best friend who has now become my mentor, couple friends that Joe and I have inherited who have been there through it all, work friends who have become framily and stayed even after we've all left the job, so many people I met on my road to public service who just stuck. I have "girl gangs" and "wedding friends" and so many people who fed into me and supported the writing of this book.

I have a whole group of amazing female writers in my circle who are my inspiration and my source of strength and wisdom as I embarked on this journey. This book would not have been conceived or birthed without you. Thank you.

Colleagues & Coworkers.

As this book reveals, I have worked in many places and in many spaces, and because we spend more waking hours at work than at home, it goes without saying that there are people whom you spend time with at work who become your framily.

To every person who has ever given me a chance or a job, encouragement and advice, been a sounding board or free focus group, shared a drink with me on a Friday (or a Thursday, or really any day that ends in -day) to celebrate an accomplishment or just the end of a long week, you are a part of the fabric that is me. Thank you.

Cheerleaders and Encouragers.

Thank you to every single person who ever volunteered or worked on my campaigns, who voted for me, encouraged me, and prayed for me. Thank you to anyone who ever watched me on television and who wrote an encouraging word to me via email and social media.

We are a product of all of those experiences. On any day, it may be the thing that helps you get through a tough moment or a seemingly impossible day, week, or year. As I get older, I realize that gratitude is a reciprocal energy. You receive as you give it.

So know that I am grateful for every single person who has been a part of my life and my story. This book is dedicated to each one of you. Thank you.

Printed in the USA
CPSIA information can be obtained
at www.ICGtesting.com
LVHW060625070823
754494LV00001B/188